While I Was Out . . .

My Near-Death Experience
&
Soul Altering Journey

Deirdre Dewitt-Maltby

While I Was Out . . . God Came In
My Near-Death Experience

Deirdre Dewitt-Maltby

. . . God Came In

Table of Contents

The two sisters -
Dea and Sandy.

Sandy giving
Dea a hug.

A Sister's Words

I have believed in miracles for a long time… In November of 2008 I was a first-hand witness to several of them.

miracle (noun) 1. An event that appears inexplicable by the laws of nature and so is held to be supernatural in origin or an act of God:

"Then Jesus said to him, Unless you see signs and miracles happen, you never will believe (trust, have faith) at all."
- John 4: 48

I believe that we overlook miracles on a daily basis. And, sometimes, God has to speak loudly to get our attention.

This book is the account of my sister's story, as she was a participant in the most wonderful miracle of all. She was held in the palm of God's hand and felt His unconditional love in a very personal way. A way that has changed her, or should I say, has answered a lot of her questions, and helped her find her true self.

On November 18, 2008 a horrible automobile accident started a chain of events that sent ripples into many lives, probably more than we can actually account for. The following pages are my sister's own words and journal about the events during her odyssey and subsequent thoughts and experiences. It's an amazing journey, to say the least … One that has brought my sister to a place of peace in this world of confusion.

I know she would have liked to stay in the paradise she experienced, but I'm thankful she's still here with me.

Sandy Lyles

enough by this book to stir something inside of them. If this happens it is God doing the touching . . . he's only using me to get through to you. So if I never meet you or get a chance to speak to you, please know that I am so grateful for the opportunity to have shared with you in some small way.

God, Spirit, whatever your name for the Creator is, works in many ways to touch our lives. My hope is that, for you, this is one of them.

Thanks you for letting me share.

Dea

THE LAST THING
I WAS DOING

The last thing I was doing was looking for God. For me it was just an ordinary day, and I certainly wasn't doing anything that could even remotely be considered a spiritual quest. In fact, I was happily planning for the Christmas holidays ahead. I was enjoying a few days of shopping for our antique store and a bit of time off to be with family. Little did I know, that fall day, what awaited me. Little did I know the "me" I had always known, was about to die.

For the past thirteen years I have made my home in the small, remote, and breathtakingly beautiful mountain town of Salida, Colorado. I moved across the country from South Florida with my husband Daniel and son Brendan to this quaint town just east of the Continental Divide. My only sibling, Sandy, also brought her family to Salida at the same time. My sister and I, as well as our husbands, were making mid-life changes, starting our new lives in a new town. We all felt Salida was a good choice for a place to live and to finish raising our respective families.

Before this move to Salida my life, as a whole, had been quite full and rewarding, both in business and social endeavors. I have always been a hard worker at whatever my undertakings and, I am proud to say, I have been happily self-employed for most of my working years. After college in New York City I left my chosen field of fashion design and ran, along with husband Dan, our own commercial design studio for almost fourteen years in my hometown of Fort Lauderdale, Florida. Then, after moving to Colorado, I changed gears and together with my sister began to delve into the world of antiques. Running both the commercial design studio in Florida, and later the antique business in Colorado, was more of an act of love than the drudgery of real "work". And, even though the ups and downs of my life have been numerous, I always have felt that I was still a pretty "together" person. I have always been a person who has been active, able to adapt, and willing to try new adventures.

The story I share is of an experience that came from out of the blue - an adventure for which I was not prepared, to say the least. On an ordinary day, in the natural course of living, a near-fatal car accident became the turning point of my world. My life, my way of thinking, and my very being was transformed in ways that I never would have imagined. Those changes are ongoing to this day and part of what I will try to convey with these writings.

I'm not a professional writer and I'm not really sure how to start these pages. In fact, communicating any of my important thoughts and experiences – any of my interior life - has always been difficult for me. Now I am attempting, as best I can to bare to the world and transform into the concrete form of written words, my thoughts and experiences of a very private nature.

How does one describe the indescribable or speak of concepts that seemingly cannot be said with mere words? How does one accurately put into words the account of such an unexpected spiritual journey? Yes, words do fall short, but I will do my best to convey how God or Source reached me, and what crossing over to another realm of existence was like.

I have given a lot of thought as to why I have felt strongly compelled to share my story. My life has been so altered by this incredible and totally unexpected journey of the past year. I view this experience as a gift. It is a gift I can share with others and, perhaps, it may also be of some benefit to them. Perhaps either my experience or subsequent journey of thoughts will resonate with someone so they will not feel so isolated in their own lives. Not only have I wanted to share my adventure, but my heart knew and was somehow told, that this sharing would certainly happen.

I must admit that I am also writing this story to help clarify my thoughts. Seeing my thoughts transformed into words on a page somehow validates what I feel within. It also strengthens my resolve to share these intimate experiences. This written account of the accident and my ongoing, unfolding, spiritual journey is helping me work through it all. It is helping me to clarify my own understanding of the nature of God. It is helping me clear my vision of how I even understand the term "God".

But without ever being written on any page or paper, my experience is forever etched upon my heart. It will be my guide to whatever future I may be graced to have.

Included here is just a bit about myself and childhood, to give you a brief glimpse of me and who I am, with some of my simple perceptions of my life. I was raised in what I would call an average American home. My mother and father were practicing Presbyterians. Our family unit consisted of only four - mom, dad, my sister, who was four years my junior, and me. I had what most would consider the traditional Christian family upbringing, with church and Sunday school attendance as well as the social interactions and values that accompany this type of life.

I certainly felt I prayed much like everyone else. In my prayers I was always hoping that this God I was learning about would hear me. I hoped that God would help, and sometimes I certainly felt he did. Yet somehow, as I was growing up, I never felt that I got the true gist of what this "God thing" was really all about.

Many times I felt as if I had been left out of a private club. I felt that others understood God better than I did. Many seemed satisfied with their understanding of God while I, for the most part, did not. While I attended church even into young adulthood, I never fully understood the workings of organized religion. In fact, religion in general did not seem to make a lot of sense to me. So going to church, for me in my early years of life, was more to meet a family obligation than an attempt at any sort of meeting or discovering this "God".

I have always had some conception of a higher power that I refer to as "God" or "Source". When I was ten years old my father died before my eyes. Watching this horrific event propelled me into experiencing what others told me were "God's ways" fairly early in life. But I still didn't "get it" or understand.

On an early, cold snow-covered morning in January, 1963 I awoke to an extremely loud noise and then screams. Running into the den at the far end of our house I found my mother kneeling over my dad. He had just somehow managed to pull the trigger of one very long shotgun, in an attempt to end his own life. (My dad had cancer and they feared it had gone to his brain.) Having no pillows for his head I sat on the floor cross-legged and cradled his head on my lap. Looking down at his face, which was upside down from my viewing perspective, I watched as the life drained from his eyes. I looked up with a million questions in my mind to a panic stricken mom. *"What -o - what was happening??!!!"*

In 1963 ten year-olds were still pretty much "kids," unlike the worldliness of some ten year-olds of today. In my middle-class security and protected innocence I didn't know much about the concept of death. (Unless you count the goldfish I saw die when I was 6 as he took a jump to the carpet from his little fish bowl on my dresser) Nor did I know how the loss of my father in such a traumatic way would utterly change my life or the outlook I would have on the world as I grew.

I was told it was "God's Way" that my dad died the way he did, and that if I asked God he would make me understand . . . but I certainly didn't at that point. Even though our church minister was quick to respond to this family tragedy, whatever "God" he kept talking about, was lost on me. I seemed lost to myself from that point on, and would be so for many years in the future. And even though my asking never stopped, God never seemed to send me any answers to much of anything.

So because of, or in spite of my childhood trauma, I looked into many spiritual or self discovery paths over my young and adult years. Only a few times in that process did God feel "real", "close" or "personal" to me in any way. This so called "God" had mostly remained a vague and distant concept to me. Yes, I would have to say that God seemed always to be someone or something that was "*out there*" and from my perspective, as I have stated, God did not want to communicate.

By middle-age I felt that I had still not reached any type of true closeness with the Creator, or Source, or God. I began to feel that this must be normal, and for me, at least, was acceptable. I had more of a "hope" than a belief that there might really be a God. At some point my search for this God was put on the back burner of my mind, thoughts, and ultimately my life. For me, most of the time, God was not "Knowable." Even though somewhere buried inside myself I did try to understand God, unless there was a need or crisis to deal with, my life pretty much went on without him. November 18, 2008 is the day all of that changed.

******

So the last thing I was doing was just living my life. At the age of 56 I was a happy woman, fairly pleased with her daily routine. I was a woman who without warning, was thrust into a soul altering event. The changes from this event are ongoing and in profound ways are ongoing to the present. I had a life and soul altering near-death experience. This experience did not end when I was out of the physical danger of dying, or out of my coma. My lessons were to be many in a few short weeks.

I will tell you how God made himself known to me when I was so close to death. In the second part of my story I will share the changes that my life, heart and soul have experienced and undergone since that event. My story now is a work in progress, for the learning still continues, and my life is unfolding in such wonderful and unexpected ways.

******

This experience has, without a doubt, transformed my whole being. I would have to say that this experience has re-wired my soul. I am the same me, only the direction manual for running me seems to have changed. It is like a computer that has been reprogrammed and then rebooted. I am still exploring this new way of being and getting used to this new way of being alive, this new way of "Knowing".

One of the things that became very clear to me is that I must find and grow close to God on my own. Other people can offer insight or thoughts to ponder and directions in which to look.

This last year helped me discover that God is already within my own heart, waiting, just waiting, for me to find him.

And so I share with you this story. Perhaps it may help to point you towards your own way, your own discovery of the infinite source of God that resides in you, and that I now know resides within us all.

.

JUST ANOTHER ORDINARY DAY

It was a beautiful bright and unseasonably warm fall day. I was in Colorado Springs shopping for Christmas accessories and other goodies to bring back to sell at the antique emporium I own with my sister Sandy.

The day before, November 17th, I had driven to Colorado Springs from my mountain home to take my mother-in-law, Barbara, and her friend, Linda, to the airport. They had been at our home with Dan and me for a wonderful and loving week. Most of that week is gone from my memory now, but the essence of the good feelings we shared remains. After dropping both women off mid-afternoon at the airport, I spent the rest of the day in the city shopping for our store. I was also waiting for evening, and a planned dinner date with my son.

I often met 28 year-old Brendan for dinner when I made the hundred mile trip from my Salida home to the city. Many times he would offer his house so I might spend the night if I needed to get more shopping done the next day.

We had a fine dinner that night. For some reason we chose a place neither of us had ever gone to before. It was also a bit more expensive than our usual dinner haunts. There was a special sweetness to that night; good meal, good conversation, and loving warmth. As I sat across from my son who was now a young adult I thought about how much I enjoyed his company. I thought about how proud I was of him, and what a caring man he had turned out to be. After our dinner we returned to his house and I did spend the night, excited about having those extra hours to peruse many stores the next day.

Tuesday, November 18th, was again bright, clear, and showed promise of being another balmy day. Almost having a summer's warmth to it even at early morning, the day saw me energized and ready to immerse myself in hours of shopping that were ahead of me. I dressed, pulling on a lacy top, my blue jeans, long denim duster, and of course, all the usual array of silver jewelry I'm never caught without. I had no idea that on that day, I was dressing for the adventure of my life, a life, that internally, would never be the same again.

By mid-afternoon I finished treasure hunting for our store. My loyal, and ever-present, canine companion Reebok, had come on this trip to the big city with me - "mom". In fact, my wonderful greyhound-dobie mix pooch can usually be found with me 24-7. He is part of the canine greeting committee down at the antique store, and loves accompanying me on all my shopping excursions. In fact, this dog is so much a part of my daily life that those that know me, know that if they see me he is not far away and vice versa. I remember letting him have one last potty run, and a few more minutes of sniffing and meandering in the grasses next to the parking lot of my last stop. Leaning against the car I watched him and let the sun warm my face, enjoying those moments. Important necessities taken care of, he and I were on our way - me, dog and store goodies - in my husband's Tahoe. We wound our way through the city and set our sights for the mountains and home.

A bit after 3 p.m. I called Brendan to thank him for the previous night's dinner company, comfy lodgings, and for being such a wonderful son. I gave him the usual mom/son "kiss" over the phone and told him that dad would be quite surprised to see me back home so early. Shopping trips to the front range usually saw me back in Salida very late at night. Dan often turned in well before I ever got home and let myself in the house.

My son agreed that his dad would definitely wonder what was wrong with me for leaving Colorado Springs well before dark and foregoing many hours of shopping to return home. We laughed over this, and said our goodbyes.

As I headed south on Highway 115 and away from Colorado Springs, I knew within a few miles I would lose cell phone reception and not be able to call anyone, so I quickly called my sister to check in with her, and to see how the day had unfolded at our store.

According to the phone records, we would review later, we had only talked a little more than one minute before getting cut off. Instead of calling her back I tried my husband's cell number but somehow got it wrong and so I hung up. Only mere seconds of my old life remained, yet how could I have known?

I left the city and was a short way out of town when I crossed a small bridge before starting up a hill. Just past that bridge the road on my side opened up from one lane into two. I edged my car over to the slower right lane to let the cars behind me pass.

What happened next was so quick I didn't have time to think about what was going on. The right front tire of the Tahoe went off the road on to the right shoulder and I heard an extremely loud bang or thud. Had I experienced a blow out? The car was pulled to the right very dramatically. Steering the vehicle back on to the roadway, and before I had time to assess the situation further, I realized my car was fish tailing wildly. I looked up and saw that I was headed in the direction of oncoming traffic. Not one, but two semi trucks were racing down the hill towards me and I was swerving towards them.

It is amazing how time can seem to both speed up and slow down at the same instant. I saw one large semi passing by me in the opposite direction so I knew my car would not collide with that one. The next truck, however, was in my path. I estimated that at best the Tahoe would graze the semi's front left fender but still be the cause of what was sure to be a horrific chain of events. Following very close behind that oncoming truck were two passenger vehicles. In a flash I realized that these cars would be involved and that I would not be the only one to lose my life. I saw death. That death, or its closeness, brushed its hand across my soul. I had time to feel how immensely overwhelming and horrible a feeling this death seemed to be. I truly felt my life was going to end. I remember thinking: "NO – *NOT LIKE THIS!"*

I felt that everything was in slow motion. And I was seeing every detail yet I knew it was happening in an instant. My next response, however, was not slow. I thought, in that instant, that I was steering the Tahoe back over to the right side of the road. I must have turned the steering wheel too quickly as the car continued to swerve for it caused the vehicle to turn perpendicular to the road itself, sending it careening up the embankment on the right-hand side of the road. The momentum sent the car into a roll. Part of me could not believe what was happening, the other part just watched in frozen horror . . . and hung on.

I was traveling about 55 mph. Within this crazy instant I heard my mind say "tree or bush". Even though I have no memory of any trees or bushes along the side of the road, I guess this is what I was hoping to hit as I left the pavement, instead of any other vehicles. Just before turning the car that last time I also remember thinking that I did not want to kill anyone. "Please let it only be me who dies in this accident." Within a blink of an eye it was all over. In reconstructing the accident the EMTs believed that the car rolled two and a half times before hitting the embankment.

I don't know how long it took me to collect my thoughts, but I know I did not lose consciousness. I became aware that the car was no longer moving and got an up close and personal sight of a mountain of earth pushing its way into the front windshield of the partially crushed car. Cubed fragments of glass surrounded and rained down on me. It was only then that I realized I was hanging upside down within the vehicle. My very first thought was "Oh NO! This is NOT good, Dan's not going to like this at all!" Then I got the crazy notion that perhaps passers-by could turn me right side up, and maybe send me on my way again. I could deal with the windshield when I got home. It was unrealistic thinking to be sure! I had no idea I had totaled the car. It would, of course, never be driven again, let alone make the trip back to Salida.

Next I heard a loud and continuous noise almost like an airplane engine. It was the car, still running, growling very deeply, but going nowhere. My mind was in a weird state of numbness. All of a sudden I heard sounds from behind me. It was the crunching of bags and glass and I was filled with dread. For those last few seconds I had completely forgotten about Reebok. My dog was climbing over broken glass and plastic shopping bags that had been in the back seat, but were now on the inside rooftop of the overturned Tahoe. He was scrambling out one of the windows that had blown out on impact. My heart panicked. I was upside down and could not get a mental handle on what was happening to me. At the same time, I was afraid that the next sound I heard would be that of screeching tires and a loud thud as Reebok got hit. The fact that the road had lots of traffic at that time of day was still very fresh in my brain. I called for Reebok, loudly, over and over again, but he did not return to the car. My only concern was for him - that dog is like my child - and at that point I was in a state of terror.

After yelling his name as best I could for what seemed like many moments, he still did not return. It was then I realized I had to figure out what was happening to me. What was this situation I was in? I had to concentrate, to focus. I wanted to free myself, of course, but I couldn't move. I was stuck in a very tight upside down position. This claustrophobic condition sent waves of panic through me – I was certainly not going to be able to get out on my own.

It's amazing what we focus on in times of emergencies. I noticed the sandy brown color of the dirt that was my view out the now nonexistent windshield. My hands were somewhere above the front of my face, still hanging on to the steering wheel, or hanging on to something, their color a muted fleshy pink. Dark red blood was dripping from them where the glass had made its cuts. The blue denim jacket I was wearing was catching this blood from below, the jacket staining a very dark, almost black, color, where the blood fell. I felt so disconnected from all this. I wished the past few seconds of life could be rewound somehow. I wanted a do-over and perhaps things would be different, better than now.

People came to my aid within seconds after the crash. They were pulling on the car door to try and get it open, but it would not budge. A man on my left took hold of my hand, and was telling me to take slow, deep, easy breaths. He also told me that the EMTs were on their way. For one brief moment I stopped noticing my panicked heart and listened. Sure enough, I could hear the sirens in the background and I felt relieved. But I still could not believe any of this was real. I should be many miles up the road by now. Why was I not happily finishing my afternoon drive home? Why was life now out of control for me? . . . *Why?*

Since the people gathered around the car could not get the door open I was stuck in my upside down position. My head was being pushed down into my chest, and the weight of it all was on the back of my neck. The pressure was now getting stronger with each passing second. I heard voices telling me it wouldn't be very long for help to arrive. The EMTs would be able to get me out of the car.

At first I was not scared, but shortly, I felt a type of panic I had never known before. I knew that if they did not free me quickly from the car, my neck would snap in its present position. My mouth was starting to fill with fluids, I was choking, and the pressure on my neck was becoming close to unbearable. I screamed, as best I could, for them to hurry. The colors were fading from my vision and I knew I only had a few more seconds of consciousness before I would succumb to the blackness that was rapidly closing in around me.

In what seemed like the next instant, after hearing many voices and much commotion, the door swung open and I was slid out gently onto the roadway and freedom. Feeling small pebbles that lay along the side of the road, and which were now beneath my back, gave me a feeling of security. I was now staring up into the most beautiful soft blue sky I had ever seen. I felt firm skilled hands lifting me, as I was being turned on my side and laid back down on the backboard that was now under my body. As the paramedics worked over me I let my hands fall off that backboard and onto the ground. My hands again felt the pebbles and I savored the feeling of their texture. It meant that I was still alive and could touch, could feel. This somehow gave me a small bit of temporary comfort.

I was still able to speak and I kept pleading with those around me to find my dog. "His name is Reebok, and I'm not leaving without him!" I did not care what happened to me, I just knew that if they let me up for just a few minutes, I could call him back! Then they could take me to the hospital if they really felt I needed to go. In the background I could hear voices calling for him - bless them! It must have been a few of the stopped bystanders calling his name. Of course the paramedics ignored my pleas. They ignored this crazed lady on a wooden backboard in the middle of the highway, trying to somehow call for her dog! At that time I had no idea as to the extent of my injuries. I did not know they felt I might even die right there on that road. I am grateful for that ignorance.

BRIGHT LIGHTS AND
A SENSE OF CALM

The emergency crew slid me into the ambulance. My chances of getting my dog back were now completely gone. I had no control over anything in my life now. What a shocking, foreign feeling, to be completely helpless.

Inside the ambulance my first sight was of the recessed lights in the ceiling of the truck. I remember looking up at them and focusing on the strength of their brightness. I don't know why I did this. Perhaps I needed to ground myself. Staring at the light seemed to keep me focused. My mind was reeling yet I was trying hard to stay in the present moment.

Over and over my thoughts returned to Reebok and the panic returned. There were fences and steep hillsides where I crashed. How could any dog survive being abandoned on such a busy major highway with nowhere to go? There were so many trucks out there going by at 60-70 miles per hour!

All of a sudden, and out of the clear blue, I found myself pleading to God. If God was out there, if he had made my dog, then he could control the circumstances and keep Reebok safe until someone could find him. There was only one prayer, *"God, keep my dog safe. You are the only one who can do it."*

In the instant after my plea it was as if the light from that ceiling fixture came down and entered into the front of my face and head. One would think that this would be a startling or frightening feeling to have. Light entering one's body is certainly a bizarre and unexpected thing. Yet it was not at all unsettling and seemed to be happening as a natural course of this experience and the past many moments.

This light then went down the length of my body. As it traveled, down and through the inside of my body, the light became feeling, and that feeling was one of an indescribably soft peace. I was acutely aware of being able to observe and feel this, in what I knew must be a fraction of time. As this bright light/feeling went through my body, it pushed the panic and fear ahead of it, down my trunk and into both legs. I felt the panic swiftly exit through the bottoms of my feet. I even knew that these panicky feelings traveled the short space between the end of the gurney and the back of the truck. My head was stabilized, yet by looking downward, I could see that the door of the ambulance was open about three inches. With sort of a "Whoosh" all of those feelings went out that opening; out and into the soft pale blueness I could barely see beyond the door. Then, as if on cue, I heard the door shut with a strong metallic click, leaving the panic and fear outside. Someone then thumped the door from the outside of the ambulance to let the driver know he was free to go.

As I lay there, with this soft peace filling my body, I knew that all was well; my dog, myself, everything. I knew now that no harm would come to my dog. I knew that I was going to be perfectly fine. I *was* perfectly fine. Something in my head told me to observe and just relax. It was as if an unseen someone was there with me giving words of comfort to my heart and soul. Yet no words were spoken, only safe feelings flooding my body. I was being taken care of, all was good - it really was. I surrendered to my surroundings.

There were no more prayers or spiritual thoughts from then on. The moments were going by way too fast for me to collect any sort of rational, concrete thought. While in the ambulance I was still in a state of disbelief that all this was happening to me. I felt them cutting away at my clothes. I did have silly, fleeting thoughts like, "Gee, he's cutting up my best denim shirt. I wish he wouldn't. I really like it" or "Wonder if I will still be able to get home before Dan." The paramedic must have asked me questions for I remember spelling out my last name and giving some of my medical history. I remember hoping that they were listening to me and writing this information down. I wondered too if I was reciting this information to help keep me from going into shock, to help me stay awake, to help me hang onto ME.

I knew they needed to know all about me before I slipped into unconsciousness. At one point the male paramedic asked me on a scale from 1-10 what was my pain level? Stopping to think about that for a second, I realized I wasn't really experiencing any pain, but I think I told him a "2" for I didn't know what else to say. I couldn't come to grips with the fact that while only moments before I was enjoying the mid-afternoon drive home now other people were controlling my entire life. My life was literally in their hands.

I was looking at the young man working over me, and saw that the left side of his face was scarred. Thoughts raced through my mind. Perhaps he had injured himself trying to get me out of the car. I felt terrible. I hoped that wasn't the case but I knew there was nothing I could do. I even apologized to him in my mind. (Months later I found out he had been injured in a fire years before.)

The ride to the hospital seemed to be over in a flash. Everything was happening at warp speed now. The paramedics slid me out of the ambulance and I watched, looking straight up, as they wheeled me into the hospital and down the corridor to the emergency room.

Just like those medical emergency shows on TV, I was watching the ceiling lights whizzing by with unfamiliar faces overhead. Colors, lights and noises all rushed past my gurney as we headed down the hall. Once in the emergency room I saw many more faces looking down at me as they came and went. I heard lots of voices talking, and what sounded like paper ripping, then metal instruments clanging on metal trays or tables.

Those sounds scared me. I had taken stock of myself as best I could. I thought I was fine. I couldn't imagine what they might be doing. All I could do was stare up at the ceiling, my neck in a brace, and wonder why the big hurry? I knew that everything was going to be OK - didn't they? I wanted to tell them but couldn't, I could only watch.

I don't know if they gave me anything for pain. I wasn't in pain, but I must have been slipping in and out of consciousness for I only remember bits and pieces of things. When my eyes were open I tried very hard to stay focused but that was certainly becoming more daunting as the minutes ticked by. I remember being in the CT scan machine and seeing the deep maroon band of light around the edge of the tunnel of the machine. I knew I had been in a CT scanner before and felt glad I could still remember that. I was comforted that I had some sort of rational thought and could hold onto reality. But it was getting more difficult to do by the minute.

I felt very comfortable. At some point I wondered if I was naked, or covered in any way, but didn't seem to care if I was or not. The temperature in the room seemed soothing and warm. They slid me part way into this machine, but brought me back out again, within seconds. Some man came next to my right ear and told me he was taking off my earrings, they had forgotten to do that in the ambulance. I knew about metal objects in CT scan machines – not a good thing. He softly told me what he was doing and that he would be going to my left ear as well, to remove the other earring. Being a woman who loves her jewelry, I worried about whether he would remember to keep the backs of the earrings together with the rest of them. I was hoping they wouldn't get lost. Its humorous looking back on that now, that something so very trivial was, of all things, what was on my mind at that point.

The next memory I have is being awake and hearing voices around me somewhere in the room. Through the other voices I heard my son Brendan, and my heart leapt with joy - everything would truly be fine now, family was here! I heard him talking to someone, possibly a nurse. He sounded very authoritative, and I remember feeling proud of him. Brendan came over to me, held my hand and talked with me a bit. I saw that he was holding my large Mickey Mouse carryall satchel that had apparently been retrieved from the car and brought with me. That bag goes with me everywhere, just like my dog, so seeing familiar things seemed to add immensely to my comfort level. My son, with a Mickey Mouse bag over his shoulder, and a disheveled look on his face also gave me a moment of mental comic relief, yep, everything was going to be A-ok for sure!

We talked for a short time. I could only speak in short spurts for I had to stop and inhale before speaking a few words as I exhaled. My voice was weak and raspy and my lungs shallow and croupy. I was still an observer of the frantic moments of the real world which swirled around my inner calm. By this time I had been transferred from the Emergency room up to ICU but must have been slipping in and out of consciousness for I don't remember the trip.

While Brendan was holding my still bleeding hand, a doctor came and told me that I would need to be put to sleep for a while, as I was bleeding into my lungs. I remember seeing someone over me and I agreed to whatever was wanted. I squeezed my son's hand. I told him I loved him and asked him to tell Dan and Sandy that I loved them as well. I felt I would be awake by the time they got to me. I would then, of course, have to endure the husband-to-wife type lecture about destroying the car. It was *not* something I was looking forward to at all! They would have a two and a half hour ride from Salida to Colorado Springs, and I would apparently be put under well before they arrived. I never did have to hear that lecture!

The doctors must have acted quickly, for I remember nothing more that happened in that room. I was transported very swiftly into sleep and what was to be another realm of life.

WHERE AM I?

Eventually I awoke. I was in some sort of void. I was not aware of my body. The only things I saw were two very bold, strong colors. The color orange was on the left, navy blue to my right. Everything had become those colors, that's all there was to see, orange and navy blue. I felt as if I was in a room with no walls, just these two colors as they surrounded me.

These colors glowed from within somehow. I noticed that where the two colors met there was a jagged edge of brown. I remember, wondering what I was looking at and wondering where I was. I thought my eyes were completely open, but seeing this was very confusing. As I looked at the point where those two colors met, that jagged line of brown, I was thinking "What the heck is this?" I had time to look at the strange surroundings, the colored nothingness that was all around me. I was able to formulate thoughts and ask myself questions. Suddenly, I was overcome with the most intense pain I had ever felt. Again the thoughts of "What is happening to me? Where am I?" I felt as if someone was picking me up by the ankles and slamming me, chest first, onto a concrete table. I never knew such pain could exist. Yet I did not feel I had a physical body, so how was I feeling this pain? Was I in the hospital basement? Were they doing terrible things to my body?

I was screaming inside myself now, hoping to be heard by the world outside this realm of orange, blue and brown. The greater the pain became, the uglier the colors became. At some point, they melted together, everything turning a gory shade of brown. I was absolutely terrified. I screamed with all my soul, hoping to be heard. The non-verbal screams reverberated through me as the pain overcame my senses. I truly couldn't stand it any longer. Then, giving up the struggle and falling into that pain, I remembered nothing more. Throughout my ordeal, this was the only real pain, or discomfort I was to ever have. It was experienced without my feeling I was attached to my body or knowing where my body was.

Later, I opened my eyes (or I thought I opened my eyes) and believed I was still in the same room I had been in with my son and the doctor. But instead, I was surprised to see myself encompassed by a breathtakingly beautiful, bright, yellow-gold light. It was very intense yet very soothing. I blinked my "eyes" but everything remained the same - a yellow-gold void. My first thought was, "How did they do that in this hospital room? Is this some type of new way to comfort patients?"

There seemed to be a lot of time to observe this beautiful essence of yellow. When I looked straight ahead it was as if the center was a very pale yellow gold. This center was very brilliant, and illuminated. As my vision looked outward from the center, the yellow became deeper and more vivid. It was a very rich saffron, or school bus yellow color. And toward the outer rim of my "eyesight" the color turned a deep shade of orange. I have no idea how long I bathed within that color. I was what I would call conscious of my thoughts at this time. I felt awake and very rational yet this was also a highly illogical and unrealistic situation.

I could look 360 degrees in all directions and this is when I realized I really wasn't attached to my body. I was totally aware of this fact yet it did not feel strange to me in any way. In fact, I almost felt as if I was being cradled by this fantastic color. No body, just the soul, or invisible part of "Me" was being held by the color. My mind was transfixed in total fascination.

Being encircled by this radiant yellow seemed to bring me restful peace. I felt that this color was there to calm me and so it did. It flowed over me, through me and around what I knew to be the essence of "Me." This is hard to explain because I have, of course, been attached to my physical body my whole life. Feeling the ability to exist without a body is quite difficult to describe accurately. There was no tunnel or darkness, just this incredible color that became the peace inside of me, became a part of my soul. This experience is outside of time. It makes no sense to say the experience was of a certain length because, for me, it was eternal. It was part of the eternal flowing over and through "me." It was the beginning of my journey.

At some point, during my calm state, I was pulled through what I perceived to be many thousands of colors. This all started slowly, one color at a time. Each color got more vivid or intense than the last, and the colors then magically changed shade from within.

I heard sounds too and I became aware that I was hearing some type of music. Certainly both the colors and the music were quite different from anything experienced in my lifetime but it all seemed so very natural, as if it had always been like that.

The colors were not flat but three-dimensional somehow. The sounds seemed 3-D as well. The experience is close to indescribable. All I can do is use words that come close to explaining the experience. There was a far greater magnitude to the range of colors and notes than we experience in our reality I knew this to be so, and even though I found myself in awe of experiencing this I also knew it to be normal.

As my journey continued, colors, music and thoughts, all became "ONE," - and I understood how this could be. Somewhere inside the music it almost sounded like voices singing, but I couldn't tell the voices apart from the music. I couldn't tell what instruments, if any, were being played. It seemed as if a million notes were being created at once but with order and unutterable beauty and majesty.

As this process washed over me I was able to feel what each beautiful color had to offer. I flowed along within that color, feeling its depth and all the uncountable shades and hues as well. Each color also had an entire realm of distinct feelings and vibrations. Beyond words again, the closest explanation is that I somehow became one with those colors - each and every one as they appeared. And throughout all of this, I still felt like me. I certainly felt as if I was normal and conscious. I was enjoying my ride. I felt I was being taken through the whole color spectrum of the universe - the dazzling yellows, vibrant pinks, magentas, rubies, scarlets, rich crimsons, sapphires and a zillion shades of blues whirling into purples and greens.

The colors also became patterns, much like that of very complex computer designs, and as enticing as that of an intricate kaleidoscope. I could see these patterns as a whole, or focus in on a small, detailed part of them. It was fascinating, incomprehensible, but completely normal.

Complex plaids and other patterns wove themselves together with infinite details - they seemed to have a purpose. I saw and understood them all. I could move into them and become a part of these designs and weavings. Then I experienced a simple and profound revelation - through this experience of colors and sounds or, perhaps, because of it, I could somehow understand the complexity of life, of Source, of God. I wish everyone could have this experience because it is not something that words accurately convey. It is simply beyond description in this realm while still seeming so understandable and normal in this other realm of existence I found myself in.

The unearthly but stunningly fascinating music I heard seemed very far away yet simultaneously seemed to be running through me. I wondered how this could be possible. It was far beyond anything I can now even begin to describe. I was trusting and very childlike as I watched and listened with great awe. I felt safe, utterly loved, and completely at peace with these surroundings. All existence seemed to be the colors and the intertwining music. My mind had never been as expanded or filled with knowledge as it was in the middle of this experience. With no thought of the body I left behind I was completely enthralled by this magical cosmos that was both around and within me. I was totally unbounded. I now felt as if my soul was merging with the Universe.

At one point I wondered why the color white was not a part of this spectacular lightshow I was experiencing. Having been an artist most of my life the absence of white was very apparent to me. Then, in an instant, as if someone had read my mind, it was made known to me without words that at this point I was not to see, or perhaps I should say go "to" the white. Yet, I was allowed to "feel" where it was. As I explored this feeling I could tell that it lit up all the colors I was seeing, from somewhere within, or behind them. I also could tell that it was above these colors where I was now.

This all-encompassing "Whiteness", that I felt rather than saw, went out to each side as far as forever and as high as that forever too. This white was totally pure, blindingly brilliant yet felt very welcoming. It was pureness itself, in a raw and ultimate form. It *WAS* the center of the Universe. Once again words fail to describe this in full. Feeling it though left me in total awe. I knew it was a place to which I would someday return. But for now it was within the realm of fantastic colors that my soul would be held and I was content with this knowledge.

When I made an effort to analyze or understand what I was experiencing - as I searched for meaning - it was as if a soft gentle hand, like that of a loving parent, would stroke the left side of my soul and whisper to me "Let Go - Just Be." That was all I needed to do. That was the only time I felt I heard actual words being spoken.

I was told again, somehow without words, that I need not ask, I need not know. I was safe, I was loved . . . I *was* just to "Be." For the first time in my entire life, I experienced what that was like. I am still in awe of how profound this was yet utterly simple. When I allowed myself to just "Be" another layer of understanding came into my soul. It washed over me like a soft flowing liquid of energy and light.

I could have been there for a few minutes, hours, or a thousand years, it would have been the same feeling. Time did not exist. It was as if the colors just opened up to the universe beyond. I saw and felt the wonders of the cosmos. I could see into eternity, see the entire Universe. The past, present, and future all were one. I could feel the essence of every soul that had ever existed, or ever would. I was a million miles away from any earthly home I had ever known. ***Yet this was home!***

This is so difficult for me to accurately convey but at some point came the understanding that I was being allowed to "Know." If I had access to write what I felt I knew at the time, it would fill volumes. As quickly as one truth flowed though me there was another insight. Yet at that point, there was plenty of time (although all was timeless) to absorb and know (in that realm) what I was learning. I knew I was drifting through the cosmos, seeing the infinite as it is. I was understanding it "All". I was connected to it "All", while "self" was still intact. Sometimes I would drift slowly through this kaleidoscope of knowledge and colors before me. And then suddenly, I would be whisked away to another color or another thread of the weaving of thoughts. These thoughts would be beyond my comprehension here in our realm. But where I found myself in the experience, I seemed to fully understand. It was as if the universe and Creator keep nothing hidden, and is there for all of us to understand in equal measure, yet by itself is totally measureless.

I am not at all sure when I first noticed this, but I do remember that many times while I was in my coma experience I would see a huge eye looking at me, or just looking. I felt that it was peering through the colors and the patterns. Sometimes I would see it quite clearly as an eye. Other times I would just know that it was there, and observing everything from behind what I was being shown. This was so strange to me at first. I even remember feeling fear, but then a warm calmness let me know everything was okay. It looked much like the impersonal eye on top of the pyramid that is on our American currency. Eventually I felt that it was like the watchful eye of a parent making sure all was well. So bizarre, yet by this point I was finding things to be just a matter of fact or how things should be.

Early in my experience I thought I must be watching what the doctors had created with drugs to entertain me or keep me calm. I was able to think rationally and logically. But I found it was easier to "Be" as I had been instructed to do, and just watch what unfolded before my "eyes".

I never once doubted my existence, yet the self, as I know in this world, was gone and not a part of my thoughts. The body I had lived in for more than 50 years was easily left behind. I did not worry about dying because I now understood that there was no death - there just "IS". I still had the "Me" that is self, yet I easily understood becoming a part of the "All" of existence. My mind and heart were being taught things that I still have not been able to form into words. But my "Beingness" now knows that they are there, within me, waiting for discovery.

There never was, for me, the experience of seeing or going down a tunnel as is reported in so many near-death experiences. There were no borders to cross, as I just seemed to be a part of the "All" that was being shown to me. The most awesome fact was that at the core of all this feeling, knowing, and understanding was a great Love. Greater than the heat of a million suns was the magnitude of its being - Amazing! I saw that life never ends, it only moves on. Yet even in this moving on, we still carry self, we still exist in spirit. We are a part of the "All." I was somehow allowed to see "Me" as I am seen by the creator. Even now tears find their way to my face each time I recall how I saw the beauty of my soul, the beauty of all human souls.

I lost any notion of myself as unloved or less than perfect. I was able to set my questioning mind aside, to become one with the energy, the love, the light. Like the small trusting child I had become, I reached up to take the hand of the loving universe surrounding me.

I seemed to understand that this ultimate love that was being given to me came without judgment of any kind. It didn't matter what I had ever done, said, or been in the earthly world. I was still worthy of this indescribable love. LOVE was the Creators gift to me. I became aware that even as humans who are so far away from the light of perfection we are still loved. Perhaps there is judgment in some way but I was made aware that each person is free to choose where they wish their internal selves to be. We will still be loved no matter what but we will find ourselves in an existence at the level of light and understanding that has been our choosing. We will choose to exist somewhere from the brilliant light of complete understanding to the complete darkness of ignorance with all the uncountable layers in between. We choose.

Most of the "other realm" knowledge that I experienced, was mine to experience there, but not retain in this existence. And, indeed, once back in our reality it became only a vague but familiar feeling within my soul. It would, however, become something I can now only call - my "knowing". It was far beyond what is perceived with the minds we use on this plane of existence. Nor can we understand it in its entirety while in this realm of earthly living.

The knowledge I experienced was unlimited. But like a small cup cannot contain an ocean full of water, I cannot hold all that knowledge in this limited self. The drops of water in that small cup though contain the full essence of the ocean. And I have the feeling that my self does, actually, contain it All. Understanding is unfolding as needed and seems to cause my mind to grow. My cup then seems to increase to hold the more knowing and understanding that flows into it.

These words seem completely inadequate to explain what I experienced. It simply isn't possible to pull that information into this limited sphere of existence. It is frustrating to feel that I am on the verge of an explanation, that the knowledge is complete within me but I cannot express it. I cannot fully pass on the information or total experience. When something is so sweet, so clear, so delightful it cries to be shared but in its entirety it cannot be.

For me now there is no need for words to validate my experience. My experience resides within my soul and that is enough. The reality of my experience is, in some ways, more certain to me than the reality of this existence. I am certain that everyone will have this type of experience when they return to the "All, that is God. The existence beyond our earthly shell is what is truly real.

This experience seemed to have rewired my complete perception of life. I was changed in a fundamental way that is inclusive of but beyond my physical self. Though I cannot recall all the knowledge presented to me, the experience of the knowledge forever changed the core of who I am.

Just like Alice going through the looking glass, I cannot fully return to that realm in this lifetime. It will, however, always dwell within the depths of my soul. And at times, perhaps for an instant, I can briefly touch it once again. How could the "Me" I once was ever be the same again after feeling all of this?

THE TEXTILES OF THE UNIVERSE

And so my journey seemed to continue. Once I seemed to understand the magnitude and awesomeness of creativity, something spoke softly into my soul. Then I became aware that I was being given the mental "joy stick" of my own imagination. How strange a concept that seemed to be! The colors and patterns that I had watched as they were created before me were now turned over to me to make into my own creations. It was amazing - whatever I thought became vision and swirled around me in its own reality. I realized my unlimited potential as a human. I had the potential to create beauty, in thoughts, in words, and in deeds. I saw the ultimate potential of all humans and how limited we are - basically by our own actions. I let go and in the letting go it was as if my self, as an ultimate human, emerged. I was co-creating with God. I was not anywhere near the magnitude of God but was one with that force. I understood what co-creating with this unlimited force meant. The creativity of God was flowing through me and the feeling was indescribable. This is just my feeble attempt to somehow put all of this into words.

One of the great desires of my life was to have been a clothing designer. It was what I went to college to learn to become. It seems a funny, trivial thing compared to the awesomeness that I found myself in but something told me to do what I had always wanted to do. Even though my life had gone other ways and I had never been a clothing designer, it was as if I was being prodded to try it in this new realm. Out of the colors I began creating the most beautiful garments I had ever seen. Deep rich colors of maroons, sapphire and indigo blues, textures of lush velvets beyond description were all a part of these beautiful creations and were coming alive before my "eyes." These creations were also constructed with fabrics made with those textures and patterns I had seen earlier within all the colors.

When I came "closer" to inspect my work it had all been sewn with threads of a luminous gold. This gold was brilliantly shining into my soul. Voluminous hoods, cloaks and dramatic types of clothes not ever worn by anyone of this world were coming to fruition before me. At one point figures filled these clothes. They seemed to be women gathered in a circle of silent company. The deep, dark black of what seemed like night, swirled around them. When again my mind came in for a close view, I saw these women were unseen, invisible within the garments. Yet I knew that they were there. They turned as if to acknowledge my presence but were in a world unto themselves.

It was not the clothing that I was creating that was the important fact. I knew that it was the act of the creation in itself that was most important. I knew that each soul has many gifts and our potential for creativity is endless. Nothing in creativity is trite or small. Our creativeness, no matter what the arena, and how we use it, is our gift to life itself. It flows through us from God. The act of living and "being" is in and of itself the greatest creative force. So many layers of lessons and understandings came into my mind.

There are also other memories of what I "saw" during this segment of my experience. At some point I found myself in an extremely large wide open room. It was an expansive, high-ceilinged room with what must have been very large, clear picture windows around the "walls" and ceiling. The light was streaming in from all around and above. All was bright and clear. The sky outside appeared white. A white, circular staircase descended from an invisible place above with a runway extending into the room. The floor of the room as well as that of the staircase was carpeted in a white soft textured type of material.

I knew or felt there were many others in this room but I couldn't see them. I could sense a bustling of others around me. It was a showroom. Clothing designs, my designs, were to be shown on that runway. I silently watched as these invisible models came down that staircase - their unseen hands resting on the wood railings as they walked out toward an unseen audience beyond. But what looked like a beautiful fashion show was actually so much more. I watched spellbound as the show progressed. So many meanings and concepts wrapped up in this display of artistic endeavors that he words really elude me here. Yet I realized that what I was now watching was a very profound show of beauty, creativeness and love that all humans truly have to offer, and are capable of tuning into with their hearts.

There was so much more, but so far I am not able to verbalize it all, nor do I understand the symbolism of everything I saw. I hope in time my thoughts will become clearer and I will understand their meanings. I am sure to be unwrapping this endless gift I was given for the rest of my earthly life.

So, even though I did not see other earthly figures I still did not miss or even think about being human. I did, however, realize my unlimited ability to feel love. I knew that I was being held in that love and I knew that love was eternal. I finally just somehow understood. The seed of "knowing" needs no words; it doesn't need to be justified nor can it be taken away. It just is and will always be so. I knew my life would have many uncertainties, but this new knowing had taken center stage in my being. Whether I was aware of it at all times or not, it would direct me till the end of my days. Yes, I was LOVED.

If my heart had physically been there with me, it would have been able to hold only an atom's worth of what that LOVE encompasses. At last I knew what it was like to LOVE so very unconditionally - the way that the ONE who created us LOVES. When that happened my "heart" seemed to burst open and I could feel my soul touching the essence of the unseen Creator. I was feeling the love like that of a parent who so loves its child. I felt the love of true lovers, as their hearts join and become one.. I felt the love we should all have for other life forms of any kind. Knowing that all has its place, all is loved, and all is perfect no matter what.

I felt as if all the souls of the world that had ever been, or would be, were there. Yet I saw no one, just the cosmos, the infinite of what is, . . . but I could feel them, feel the energy all those humans created. I was certainly not alone. I, we, they, were not judged. There was no judgment, only LOVE. Even in this vast and complex universe, where all of our human understanding would fit on the head of a pin in comparison to what is out there, it all seemed so simple - it all revolved around LOVE.

Within this realm of consciousness I knew how ultimately I was cared for. It was like I was being reborn with the knowledge that I already had existed, would always exists, and would, with certainty, never end. It was if I was being cradled in the arms of that loving parent who loved me beyond measure and who withheld any judgmental thoughts toward me. I was totally protected. I knew in my now open heart that what exists outside (and inside) of man is the living thinking compassionate, all-knowing force that we call God. I knew then that "God" does exist, and we are all a part of "HIM." I knew that I was loved, just as I am. All the thoughts I had ever had were open before HIM. He could see the entire realm of my soul and yet still came the LOVE. Then I knew, I WAS with God and my heart could see his majesty.

This realm beyond is nothing but LOVE. Even that word LOVE is but a whisper of whatever the word might be that would describe what is there. There was no anger or hatred or criticizing. There were none of those other emotions that we use in conflict on this earth. They do not exist in LOVE. God came to me where my heart is and loved me without reserve. How could I not fall to the feet of such a loving presence? How could I not bow my soul to the presence of who I now knew to be my Creator?

I knew that I couldn't fully comprehend what I was experiencing and that we humans would never understand to what IS. It is not for us to even begin to know in full. We are not the all-powerful beings we like to give ourselves credit for.

I control nothing but what is within my heart. I can control the choices I make even if I cannot control life as it is happening around me. It is my heart and my choice to see from LOVE or not. What happens in the world I live in is a result of this choice. Fall away from that and I fall away into a world of my own doing. That is where all the ugly stuff comes in. That is where chaos reigns. I saw that it didn't have to be so. It is not like that in LOVE. It is not like that when we live with God. I searched my whole life to find my meaning to life and here, I find, it had lived inside my heart the whole time. It never was "out there", I had just not ever seen its hiding place within my soul. If every heart in the world choose from a place of love......how very different a place this would be!

And so I was held, for almost two weeks, in a place I am now only beginning to be able to describe. I could have been there an hour, a day, or forever, it would have all been the same. I knew in this "dream" world I was in, that somehow I would never be the "old" me again. I knew I had somehow seen and experienced a part of the force we call God and been given a glimpse of the magnitude of His Love. I had a brief experience in knowing the Universe. I had, indeed received a tremendous gift. Also I had laid down thoughts about the world we now live in, and all that it entails. It became forgotten to me. I felt that I could have stayed there forever.

BACK THROUGH THE LOOKING GLASS

When I first started to come back to consciousness, I fought, with my mind, to go back. But there was some sort of wall I could not return through. It felt solid and my mind could not get back through it. I really didn't know I was becoming more aware of earthly surroundings, only that I was leaving the world I had just experienced. It was a frustrating and edgy feeling. When I opened my eyes the walls of the hospital room were glowing iridescent white. I could see the rainbow of every color within that white. But the more I focused the more that iridescent faded and became as it really was, a plain white wall. Then I saw some sort of signboard on that wall. On it, written in marker, was the date, Nov. 29. Something inside of me gave me a start as parts of my mind were returning. I could not comprehend that I had been "somewhere" since the date I somehow now remembered - November 18. Then I realized I had missed the Friday after Thanksgiving – the most important day at the store. It didn't dawn on me that I had been asleep for so long. I just couldn't make my mind work. I didn't know what these thoughts I was having were. Then I must have blacked out.

At some point my eyes opened again and I looked up to my left and saw something staring down at me. It took me awhile to realize that this form I was seeing was human. I didn't even remember what human was. I had forgotten I even had a family. I did not know who, or what, I was looking at and it wasn't until I saw a smile that the knowledge of humanness came back to me. I recognized my son, Brendan! He squeezed my hand and I was back on the other side of the looking glass. I felt the solidness of that wall up against the back of my mind and knew forward was the only way I could go, and so I returned to reality and life.

It was as if I could feel my body making the transition back into itself. I had been in a coma for twelve days. It was to be awhile before I could ever tell anyone that I had not remembered them without feeling guilty for not having any thoughts about them while I was "away". I know now that I didn't need to be concerned about my earthly family. It was not for me to do. God takes care of what we leave behind. That was a concept that seemed so natural to have.

It took me a short time to come back to this reality in all respects. One of the first things I found out is that I could not talk. I had been given a tracheotomy so I could receive oxygen and with the hole in my throat I couldn't speak. I was weak as a new born kitten, I couldn't raise my hands nor could I even hold myself upright from the waist. Geesh, that was a horrible feeling! I don't remember thinking much about all I had been thorough while in my coma. Even though it was the most dramatic and profound experience I had ever had, my mind now simply went on with what the real world had to offer. It was almost as if the experience itself had been matter of fact, unexceptional! My experience was still floating somewhere in the background of my soul waiting for my thoughts to return and my mind to start processing it all. Much like a favorite book on a nightstand waiting to be opened reread and savored in the quiet moments of the night.

For now I just seemed to be an observer, watching this hospital life unfold around me. There were respiratory doctors and therapists other doctors and daily x-rays of my lungs. The minutes seemed to float one into the other. I felt as if I was watching everything from far away. It was as if everything was weaving itself together as it should and I could see beyond the daily life into that weaving of reality from the hospital, to the city, to the world, and beyond. I was very content as the observer of it all.

Dan and Brendan worked with me at first holding up an alphabet board for me to try and communicate with them. This was frustrating on both parts. My hands wouldn't cooperate because of the effects of large amounts of drugs in my body. Whatever letter I pointed to seemed to be the wrong one. When I thought I was pointing to an N for No I would actually be pointing to a U or a Z. I just couldn't wrap my brain around why they couldn't understand me. Dan and Brendan weren't good at lip reading either. From then on I used a writing tablet and even that took quite a while to master enough so that my writing was even remotely legible. It seemed in the long run only my sister got the lip reading thing down pat!

The next day was Sunday and my sister was leaving Salida to come visit me at the hospital. Dan and Brendan had told me that my dog Reebok was safe and sound. They had found him late that first night. I remember thinking I knew he was safe and that he didn't need finding. I don't know where I must have thought he would have been - I just knew that all was okay. When Sandy arrived at the hospital she parked in the garage that was across from my hospital room window. She got Reebok out of the car and started to hold him up for me to see. But when she realized that he might fall over the balcony she stuck his foreleg out between the railings. This was my first glimpse of my beloved dog! I saw his leg being raised up and down. He was waving! The snow was softly falling on this cold, gloomy November day. Silent tears streamed down my cheeks as Dan gave Sandy the thumbs up sign that Reebok had been seen. When my sister walked into that hospital room I felt such immediate glowing warmth. As she put her arms around me in the chair I had been propped up in, it was as if the colors gold and deep ruby red were flowing around us. To me, the room was immersed in these wonderful colors. I was back, we were all together, we all cried.

Sandy told me about how they looked for Reebok in the dark of the night. They found out around 9 p.m. that he had not been picked up by anyone and was still out on the highway somewhere. Sandy knew how important that dog was to me. She felt I would die if he was not found. So she, Dan, and Brendan left my bedside to head back to the crash site in the hopes of finding the dog alive. Sandy didn't think that would be the case. Her thoughts were that perhaps they would find his body lying

52

somewhere hurt or dead because of injuries sustained in the crash. For almost two hours they looked, called, and strained their eyes to find a black dog on a black night along the busy stretch of highway. At some point in all of this she pleaded to God to lead them to his body so they would at least have closure if, in fact, he was dead.

She told me that within minutes of her plea she was somehow inwardly directed to drive back down near the crash site to look in yet another area not previously searched. Within only moments, as she stood on a high bluff overlooking the highway and my husband was down next to that highway, they caught signs of the dog. His collar was jingling in the night and Sandy knew that sound, she knew Reebok was near. Out of what seemed like nowhere Reebok came walking up the roadway toward Dan. He was now only about two feet from the side of the highway and possible death.

Dan was so afraid that if Reebok was startled he might bolt out into the road and be killed before they could snag him. Bug-eyed and obviously scared to death Reebok stopped, recognizing his name was being called, but not the dark figure coming toward him. Within a few moments, however, Reebok was back in safety and a huge "Love Fest" took place back in the car. The "pack" was together - Dan, Brendan, and Sandy along with her two dogs and, of course, a very happy Reebok! Dan said that this day brought the lowest of lows and the highest of highs for everyone involved. An ordinary day had turned upside down and everyone's emotions were depleted.

My sister also told me that early in my trauma she had set up a web site concerning my progress so others could follow and that the whole town of Salida had been praying for me. I somewhat understood what she was talking about and let her know that all was good. Salida is such a close-knit and caring array of wonderful people. I was truly amazed that so many people were sending their thoughts my way, and keeping track of my progress. She asked about what I might have felt when asleep or had I remembered anything. I wrote on my notepad that I had known God. She knew that I would tell her more when I could.

That first night of my being coherent and fully awake she showed me more of this website, of posts that my friends and others had made. Though I could only read a few of them they touched me so much that I cried. I didn't know the extent of my injuries. I didn't know the grief my family had been through. All I knew was this wonderful experience I had just encountered. I couldn't talk yet so how could I tell anyone what I had seen. I hadn't even processed it all in my mind yet. My notepad certainly wasn't long enough. Would they even believe me?

I felt very tired after coming back to consciousness for I truly felt I had been awake throughout my experience of being held within the colors and sounds. My mind, I felt, had been aware the whole time I was in my coma, it just wasn't aware within this earthly realm.

Also, the experience did not end with waking up. Apparently much more was in store for me, but I had no way of knowing this, nor was I really examining the whats or whys of anything at that point. I was just going with the flow of my situation. Each moment seemed as if they all contained special miracles.

VISIONS ON THE WALL

Over the next few days I improved to the point that they could release me from the Intensive Care Unit to the trauma step-down care; the next level toward recovery and home. I do remember, however, one of the nurses explaining to me that I would need a few weeks at that level then I would go to another level and have weeks of therapy before finally going home. My mind was racing while she was talking to me and I realized that if what she was saying was true I wouldn't be leaving the hospital until well after the first of the year. Was I imagining what she was saying? I just knew I was getting better every day and I still didn't understand how damaged my lungs had been. I felt as if nothing was wrong with me. I just felt they needed to let me go home soon.

My sister told me that after my accident she was told by a doctor that my lungs were as badly contused as they had ever seen and I may not survive. I guess things had looked quite bleak for me for quite awhile. But that's another story for I was never aware of family, friends, or doctors during my coma. She also told me that after a few days they had to actually bring me up and out of a drug-induced coma as my body was not handling the strong drugs I was given and a few times I bottomed out because of them. For the rest of the duration of my sleep I was kept sedated with only enough pain meds to keep me under and manageable so that I would not waken and try to pull the life support tubes from my body.

On the afternoon of the first day in my new room I had been watching TV for a bit. It was mid-afternoon and the skies were overcast and a dingy gray. This made my room rather dark but since I was alone watching the TV it didn't seem to matter. I wasn't thinking much about anything, just watching the mindless kind of shows that are on television that time of day. For some reason I turned my head, something caught my eye to the left. As I turned my head to look I suddenly saw the darkened wall to the left of the TV come alive before me. I saw my whole life in vision on that hospital wall. The pictures weren't strong or vivid like actually watching TV, but they were there somehow and I could see them, feel the feelings that accompanied them - very strange.

It was not just my whole life but that of each of my parents. The pictures included a time before I was born as well as my life. I felt the feelings that each picture carried within it; how I or others felt at the time. I saw so many things that I had long forgotten. I saw grade school. I saw people I knew. I saw moments from long forgotten days of my life. I saw how they wove together with all the other parts of my life and other people's lives; how they were all meant to be. It was very hard to grasp all of this as it was going by so very quickly yet I knew I was gaining some sort of understanding about what was happening, and what was being shown.

My mind could not keep up with all the dreamlike visions, thoughts, and feelings flashing in front of my mind. With great speed it all happened, and all of a sudden the visions and feelings became one and it was as if the whole thing came off the wall and rushed from there invisibly into my chest. I was wide awake, not on any drugs, and observing this whole thing. At that moment I knew that my life had culminated to exactly right where I was supposed to be, and all was well. It was almost as if it was a confirmation of some of the feelings I had while in my coma. I lay back against my pillows and felt so very glad to be alive. I don't know how long I lay there feeling my breaths go in and out, listening to the steady whoosh of the stream of oxygen at my throat, but I was totally at peace, I was totally happy.

ROCKY BALBOA, ANGELS, AND ME

Later on the night of my first day in trauma step-down care I wrote on my signboard to the nurse my request to have dinner with my son down in the cafeteria. I had just been put back on a solid food regime, but still had the tracheotomy tube in my throat and was eating little. She said I was too weak to be wheeled down there and if something happened to me, or I wasn't able to breathe, they wanted me close to help. The thoughtful nurse did however, put a cute little "Reserved" sign on one of the small tables on the trauma floor, so that when my son came after his work hours we could dine at our own private table outside my hospital room. I thought that was so sweet of her to think of that. Brendan had either been going to the cafeteria to eat or bringing his food up to the room and dining from his lap. So on that Tuesday night, I was still able to have my usual dinner date with my son. It was great, and made me feel as if I was coming back to life again. Even if I was hooked to an oxygen tank and could hardly hold my body up, and everyone passing by on that floor could see my weak, feeble body attempting to function, I loved every minute of it!

The next day, Wednesday, I awoke very early when they came in to do the daily blood work around 4 a.m. and I just couldn't get back to sleep. Around 5:30 I got up and decided to do a bit of therapy walking to strengthen my body. I did the usual shuffling steps around the nurses' station, pushing my oxygen tank, and dragging another pole on wheels behind me. I still felt enough energy for more, so set off on an adventure of discovering what the rest of that floor had to offer.

I managed to find the therapy room and after trying several doors found an open one and went in. I shuffled around the room trying to use some of the things they had for rehabilitation; small steps or platforms, etc. How weird it felt to try and do even the simplest of things again, like go up and down those slight steps. But eventually, having mastered them and feeling really good about it, I looked around the room to see what else I might conquer at this early hour. I saw a treadmill and headed over to the corner of the room where it stood, silently daring me to come near. It took me a few minutes to arrange my array of hospital paraphernalia, and arrange my tubes so I did not get caught up in them while on the treadmill.

I floundered with the settings, but once figured out, set the machine and was on my way. Huffing and puffing the tread was going at a snail's pace because of my inability to get it going very fast with my feet. I set off to see how far my weakened body could take me. The course of the digital track showed it to be in quarter mile increments so this was my goal. I don't think I have ever done anything that was as difficult as this in my life. Such a normally small feat had become a monumental undertaking. My lungs were soon bursting. My body was now shaky but I was bound and determined to see those arrows close in around that track; to make the quarter of a mile loop complete. A few times I thought I might collapse. I couldn't call for help, as I still had the hole in my throat. I was becoming soaking wet from heavily perspiring. My heavy spa robe seemed to weigh a hundred pounds. It seemed to last forever but finally I saw the loop on the machine closing in on that quarter mile mark . . . 17:34 I did it! It seemed as if it had been hours! I used to run that in less than three minutes. I felt like Rocky Balboa! Shaking and wet, I made my way back, past the nurses' station and to my room. I was feeling quite good about myself!

At my room a nurse followed me in and asked where I had been. I took my sign board and wrote down what I had done and my wonderful score of 17:34, hoping that she would smile. She only scolded me and left me in my bed totally spent but totally happy. I know I must have had a silly smile on my face then. Within a very short time though, a few stern looking people entered my room. They told me the therapy room was off limits to me without a therapist. I was not to even think of doing that kind of exertion until I had built up my strength to do so. My mind is saying "Sure, whatever." I knew right then, I wasn't going to need a therapist from then on.

The next day, Thursday, was pay day for my physical exertions from the day before. I spent the entire day being weak as a kitten, barely able to hold my head or hands up. Every part of my body was shaking when I tried to do anything. I think I slept almost the whole day. Later one of my doctors came to my room. He had heard of my treadmill adventure.

I had written on my signboard as fancifully as I could "I want to go home now!" He looked at that board, looked at me, and told me that after the stunt I pulled in the therapy room I must be ready to go. If my x-rays were showing progress I would be able to go home soon. He told me that they had been very surprised at my surviving my injury and also at my recovery rate. He was also very surprised to learn from me that I had felt the whole experience to be one of the best things that ever happened to me. My doctor told me that patients usually didn't quite feel that way about their hospital adventures! I didn't go into my spiritual revelations.

Friday, my release day came and I waited happily yet anxiously for my husband to make the drive from Salida to fetch me. Reebok was with Dan and I couldn't wait to see them both. After what seemed like an eternity Dan and my beloved dog came around the corner of the hallway and into my hospital room. I was finally going home.

I feel that I have to add this incident to my story as I know that it was just one more way that God looked after me during this adventure. A small miracle that in real time or real life could have been missed or lightly passed over . . .

We were leaving the hospital and I was holding onto Reebok's lead while Dan pushed me in the wheelchair. A hospital aide was pushing the metal cart that held my many hospital accumulations. When we reached the entrance to the hospital the aide left us in the atrium and Dan went to fetch the car from the adjoining parking lot. An elderly couple came up next to me as they waited for a shuttle bus and started a conversation. My voice was weak, as my throat had recently been capped with bandages over my tracheotomy hole. I could speak but barely be heard. We were talking about Reebok and how fabulous it was that the hospital actually let animals in so they could visit their owners. Not having talked in the last three weeks I was gagging and gasping for air within a very short time of speaking with them.

Their bus arrived and I saw the man heading out to catch it. I was in an inner panic mode as I didn't think I was going to stop coughing and be able to catch my breath. The elderly lady started to follow her husband and turned to look at me she must have read my face for she waved her husband on and told him, "Hold on to your hat I'll be right back." With that I saw her go back into the hospital lobby and out of sight for what seemed like an eternity to me. I was almost ready to start flailing my arms to get the attention of an attendant or someone. *How the heck long did it take for Dan to get the car anyway? Where was he?* I knew I was ready to faint from lack of air as my coughing fit could not be stopped. I was running out of air yet I didn't want to be taken back inside for I knew that they would take me back upstairs and my chances of going home would be dashed. I, in a word, was freaking.

All of a sudden, as I had my head down trying to make it all stop so I could catch my breath, a paper cup came into view in front of me. I took the cup and lifted it to my lips - one sip of that water was all it took. My coughing fit stopped instantly. I looked up and into the eyes of the elderly woman who had been my rescuer. "God bless you," was all she said as she winked and turned to catch her husband and board the shuttle. The feelings I had experienced while in my coma came flooding back into my soul and I felt as if I had just been saved by an angel . . . perhaps I had! Time stood still for that brief moment and I saw the miracle of such moments in life.

Dan came within minutes of that incident but, being weak from it all, let it slide and said nothing about what had just happened. I doubt he would have believed my take on that story anyway. We began our two and a half-hour drive out of the city toward home. Leaving the city limits on highway115 we had to pass by the site where my accident took place. I shook inside myself, and held my breath hoping we would make it past that point in safety. Of course we did.

SUNSETS AND LOVE

It was late afternoon when we reached the outskirts of Penrose, a small town off Highway 115 on the way to our turn off road, US 50. The vistas here open up and the views are breathtaking. Mountains, valleys and flat lands all seem to merge here. The cloudless sky seemed to shine a most awesome aqua blue melting into turquoise on our left. To the right and toward the mountains was one of the most beautiful sunsets that I have ever seen in my lifetime unfolding before us. Without hesitation I bust into silent tears as I saw this. With my left hand I patted my husband's arm, and pointed with my right, "Dan" I whispered, "that is where I was, that is where I had been while in my coma, and it was even more beautiful than this sunset!"

The colors were beyond amazing, and the glow from within the sunset so very intense. It was as if God himself had painted the skies just for me to see, as we headed to Salida. I leaned back into the headrest of my seat, watching as Dan drove us toward it. All of a sudden I felt as if I was seeing and feeling myself be carried out of all those colors within the arms of unseen angels. They lifted me gently down to the earth and my feet touched the ground. It was a very real feeling that welled up out of nowhere. In that instant I knew one adventure was over and a new one just beginning. I felt myself come back into my body for good and a clarity came into my mind. There was a finality to it all.

I sat and cried and wished that my sister could see what God had just put out before me to behold. I wished that I could share that moment with her, that she would understand. As if by magic, within not even two seconds of that going through my mind, my cell phone lit up and I looked down to see I had a text message waiting for me. I lifted the phone and opened it to a screen that read: "OMG are you seeing what I am? It's awesome!" She saw too.

Later I would learn that she and others were standing outside our store in Salida watching that beautiful sunset unfold while Dan and I on the other side of the mountain, 60 miles away, were also being thrilled by that spectacular display. Sandy and I were both crying, at opposite sides of the mountain range, and thanking God for everything!

This sunset seemed to last longer than any I have ever watched. As Dan
and I headed further and further into the canyon, on the winding road following the river to home, we observed the colors deepening and changing from these brilliant pinks, yellows, and oranges, into ones of rich, burgundies, scarlets, and purples. We both spoke of how long it seemed to last. The sunset you could tell, did not want to give up its life, and hung on for almost an hour. We were almost home by the time the sky had transformed itself to night. I found out later, that many others in Salida were awed by this unusually beautiful display of color as well. Many of our friends had gone outside to observe it, some taking pictures to

record its beauty. How wonderful that this all happened on my December 5th journey back home, my journey back to a new life, my journey back to " Me. "

A BLUE ROOM, SMOKE,
AND PROMISES

Home at last, I settled in. I felt removed from it all, yet happy to be back in these familiar surroundings. My little orange kitty, "Cheetos," was more than thrilled to have his mom back. He immediately planted himself on me as I rested on the couch, purring his satisfaction at having me home. Things would go slowly, but being back, being home, was good. My recovery could now begin. Dan had even had the house fitted with my oxygen machine and a fifty-foot hose so I could go all through the house. I was still quite weak, so even walking from room to room was daunting for some time. It would be awhile for that strength to return.

It was only two days after my release from the hospital that I again had an experience that would change my outlook on life from that point on.

Early in the evening on that Sunday I was in the living room and became very fatigued. In fact, I was so tired that I told my husband I needed to go to bed. I remember kissing him goodnight. He helped me to the door of my bedroom and then he, too, headed for his room. I no sooner had I gotten into my bedroom than I became so sleepy I couldn't even get into the bed all the way. I fell across it sideways, lights on, and apparently, fell into an immediate deep sleep.

When I "awoke" I found myself in some sort of room. I thought it was a hospital room but everything around me was a deep sapphire or midnight blue. I looked up and realized a nurse of some sort was holding my left forearm - she was taking care of me. I wasn't quite sure what she was doing and I could not "see" her, as she was the same color blue as everything else. Yet I definitely knew she was there. She relayed the fact to me that there was one more procedure to be performed. I then became scared as I knew that I had left the hospital, knew that I was back at my home . . . so where was I now? In some way I knew this was a dream, but it certainly felt more real than any dream I have ever had.

In the next instant I found myself on some sort of surgery table, in an operating room. The table was soft, like a bed, and covered in white sheets. I too was covered with a white sheet, as if lying down for sleep. I could not see this as we see with our eyes, but knew it to be so. Looking down the length of my body, and past the end of the bed, I could somehow tell that there were several people in that room, I think at least four. They were doctors or care givers of some sort. They too were the color of this deep midnight blue, their scrubs, their bodies as well. Somehow I knew that though the room felt very small it expanded to infinity in all directions with this deep dark blue. It almost felt like a large airline terminal. There was no ceiling in sight. The height of the room went up into forever and the dark blueness I was seeing before me.

I knew that I should not be afraid, but I was. What were they going to do now? Hadn't I already been healed in the hospital I had just been in for almost three weeks? I looked down at these "doctors" for some type of an answer and, though I could not see them, I detected that they were all now looking upward. I too looked up and into the dark blueness and unseen light that was above us. "What kind of procedure was this? Was it going to hurt?" No one said anything at this point. They just waited, continuing to look up. I looked up as well, half excepting some sort of surgical device to suddenly appear.

For what seemed like a few moments there was nothing to look at. But then, from out of that deep, dark blueness, I watched as a soft wisp of what I thought was smoke appear. I saw very long tendrils of smoke, almost like that of steam that rises from a hot cup of coffee, only this was descending down, toward us, down and down. Silently, we all watched as it floated into full view. At one point, it appeared to be about 12 feet long. It then descended from the darkness to just above my chest. Time seemed to be standing still. I watched as this delicate wisp of grey swirls was absorbed into my body between my breasts. I could feel it enter into myself and as it did a sweet, delicious peace settled into my soul. All was quiet for a short time.

I picked my head up to look down at the "doctors" again. Even though I could not discern their forms from the rest of the blueness around us I knew that they were still at the foot of my bed. Without words they parted and, after a few seconds, through the midst of them a very soft invisible liquid started to flow toward the foot of the bed and me. It was invisible because it was the same blue as everything else.

This was all so very curious. As this soft liquid entered the soles of my feet it started turning into the most beautiful and serene aqua blue that I had ever seen. It was glowing from within. The edges became this glowing, crystallizing aqua blue. As I watched the center filled with an amazing white light. It was the same intense white light that I had known was above the colors, which I had felt while in my coma. The light, too, became liquid and all of this came up through the soles of my feet and started filling my body. I felt the warmth and love as it came up my legs. Soon it was inside my entire chest cavity and I lay back, looking at the ceiling of blue above me, just feeling what all this was like. The "doctors" around me were silent. They watched and waited.

I did not have any idea of time at this point - how long the silence lasted, how long I lay there feeling what was now inside of me. I felt a presence lean in towards me and a soft voice came close to the left side of my face. Though no words were spoken this "someone" imparted to me **"This is for you, this is our gift to YOU . . . this is the YOU you were always meant to be."** The silent words seemed so very soft, I was no longer afraid, there was only the feeling of deep love around the room. I felt for such a brief instant as if I had been transported into the heart of God, and saw myself lying before me on the bed. I was feeling the love God had for me, from his perspective. This love was unconditional, this love was complete. Then, after an unknown amount of time, there was movement. It was as if my own arms came up and around me from around the bed. They wrapped themselves around me. I was overcome with the most intense emotion I had ever known. I was back inside of myself, . . . and I was loving me!

How long I lay there immersed in this new found and wondrous feeling I do not know. The doctors or caregivers around me were silent. They seemed to know what would happen to me. I felt their presence, felt their understanding. I know that they felt me cry. My tears were of happiness. My tears were my gift back to God. These tears were coming from my heart not my eyes. I could tell that everyone in that room knew that my "procedure" had gone as planned.

Something I can only describe again as "knowing" came into my being at this point. I can't even fathom all that I was "knowing". But at some point the soft "voice" imparted to me that I would never be alone again. Now I knew that I never was or had been alone. Each second of my existence would be filled by God whether I acknowledged it or not. My heart, my mind, my soul would wax and wane over the course of my life, but I would never again know emptiness. This is a silly comparison, but I felt as if my heart had just been replaced with one of those rechargeable batteries. I remember thinking that was too simple a concept, how could that be so? And I was "told" that all I had to do was ask, and from the emptiness I would be refilled. My heart would always be filled. All I had to do was ask and then it would be so. It WAS that simple.

It was also made known to me that I would be doing things I had never done before. It was a comforting thought even if I didn't know what it actually meant. But I felt confident that at some point it would be made a clearer to me.

As I lay there many emotions and thoughts went speeding through my soul. I have yet to lasso many of them for more direct observation but the crux of it all was this:

I am a worthwhile human. I do indeed have purpose in the Universe. If I learn to love others as I was being shown how to love myself, my earthly life would unfold as it should.

A human can do no more than this.

I knew, in that timeless instant I was forever changed and that my old life and heart were shadows of what I now had the potential to become - actually what I already was. I still knew I had to more firmly realize that fact. I knew the Source we think of as God comes to everyone and everything in ways that we each need in order to understand. It may take me quite awhile to come to terms with this in my earthy life, but I knew that my soul already somehow completely understood. They operated on me, not to take something out but to put something in . . ."Me."

After a time my eyes blinked and when I looked again I was back in the hospital room with the same nurse. She was telling me that they were getting my papers ready for me to depart for home. In a short time I would be ready to leave. I looked up and where the door should have been was the mouth of a cave, beyond that was a landscape like New Mexico hillsides. The sun was shining and I vividly remember seeing the dusty tans and sage greens of that landscape against a pale blue sky. I couldn't wait to get out into that sunshine.

I awoke in a sitting position on my bed, tears streaming down my face and onto my night shirt. As I sat there in some sort of stunned silence, trying to figure out what had just happened to me, I felt as if I was not alone in the room. I felt the same loving peace that I experienced in my coma and in this "dream" I had just had. Even in the middle of this cold winter night I felt a glowing warmth surround my upright body. I felt as if silent strong and loving arms encircled both my body and soul. I was very close to the edge of that looking glass once more.

Words seem to fail me here as the feelings were so very intense and beyond my ability to verbalize. I knew, however, that what I had been shown was very real. I needed to know that and I did know that. This was not drug-induced nor a soul conjuring up a vivid dream. This was as real an experience as any in this earthly plain.

I do not know how long I sat on my bed, the experience reeling through my thoughts. I was again overcome with such great tiredness. My eyes would not stay open. I almost felt drunk. (But this was certainly not the case.) Now I climbed under my bedcovers and before I could even turn off the light I fell into another deep sleep. Apparently there was to be more.

This part is hard for me to write about let alone bring it back into memory. But I feel it, too, was a very important part of my experience so I will try my best to impart these visions and my feelings.

When I next became aware, I was standing with my arms down at my side. I found that I was in the middle of what appeared to be some sort of sludgy brown gook. There was some faint light far off in the distance which had a very faint glowing tint of yellow to it. It was almost impossible to see that light through all this muddy sea of gook. I had a brief thought that I had been encased within a cesspool of some sort. As I looked at this horrid ooze, trying to get a grip on what I was seeing, I saw that this mess undulating - it was alive. It took me by surprise but what I realized, at some heart stopping moment, is that this horrible mess was humans! I WAS in the midst of a human cesspool! Thousands, millions of humans were somewhere in the midst of that rotten stench of brown. They melted one into the other but I knew that at one time each had been separate human beings. Horror took over my soul.

As I stood there watching in complete frozen panic, this stuff pressed in on me as if to pull me into its depths. It was only then that I realized that I was encapsulated in something much like a vitamin capsule. The outer shell or membrane was very thin, like onion skin, only completely clear. This shell was so thin yet this was the only thing separating me from the horror outside. I remember raising my head to look up into the nothingness, and thinking, "Dear God, after the wonderful gift you just gave me . . . Why? WHY are you doing this to me now? What have I done to be here, please don't leave me!"

Nothing happened. I knew I was dreaming but this was not a dream, this was real. I knew that this was real in every way! The real essence of me, or what is my soul, was in this horrible place! I opened my mouth to scream but feared this micro-thin shell would rupture and I would breathe in the brown liquid horror that was trying to get to me. I was afraid when my mouth opened to scream it would rush in and consume me somehow. But, before that scream could leave my throat, I felt some unseen force snatch me up and out, back to the safety of sleep.

At some point my "eyes" again opened, I was somewhere that seemed like a large city. The odd thing was that I was now seeing everything in black, white, and shades of gray. The only color I saw from time to time was a very deep dark magenta. Magenta is a color somewhere between pink and red, but this color had a lot of black mixed in with it to make it a very dark color. I still had a faint nagging memory of where I had just been.

Though this was still not where I wanted or felt I should be, I was content to be here for the moment. I was happy to be anywhere away from that horrible mess. Now I found myself walking down what appeared to be the back alleyways of streets within this big city. For some reason I was feeling a sense of confusion, agitation and frustration. There were many people all around me but they too appeared dazed, confused and wandering with no purpose or direction to that wandering. Their eyes seemed to not really be looking at anything, they lacked life or luster to themselves. My mind felt as if it was becoming scrambled. These people who bustled by me were not bad and I was not afraid. In fact, I felt that most of them were good at heart just somehow lost or befuddled. They, too, were different shades of grey, or black and white. Occasional I would see that dash of magenta on someone, or a part of their clothing, it was all very weird. With each passing moment I was getting more confused as well. I didn't understand where I was or what I was really looking at.

A lady came up and tried to talk to me. She spoke sentences that seemed to go nowhere. Everything she said was disconnected. She certainly made no sense at all. Something in me seemed to understand her though. I have had these kinds of dreams many times in my life. I am in the middle of something very confusing, but still understand. I felt sorry that she had not pulled herself out of all this mental chaos. I tried to pay close attention to the movement of her lips to see if I could discern what she was in fact saying, I could not.

A young boy came up to me as well and the same scenario was repeated. I felt it better to just observe and not try to talk with anyone else at this point. I didn't want to be pulled into this limbo of confusion too. I looked down on the sidewalk and it seemed that the streets and sidewalks were littered with white paper flyers of some sort. I picked one up and tried to read it, but the words would not come clear to my eyesight. The words and letters kept rearranging themselves. I let it fall back to the street below. These people, I felt, though basically good, had somehow not ever found their way, they really didn't see, or find their answers in life. I did not like what I felt looking at all of this, but it did not frighten me. I only felt the frustration of knowing, they did not know. There were a lot of people here. This was a very big city. I didn't want to stay here any longer. I fell asleep again.

At some point my eyes opened but I was still within this dream I seemed to be having. I was aware that it was still a dream. This time I was out in the sunshine, and on a valley floor of some sort, almost like the one here in our valley at home in Colorado. The colors were very crisp, bold and more vivid than normal. My senses were very acute and everything seemed realer than real, if that makes any sense. I was very glad to have left the city behind. There was a beautiful clarity to being in this place.

As I looked at these new surroundings I saw people off in the distance. They appeared to be in a large group. I thought, perhaps, they were having a picnic of some sort since they were laughing and having fun. They were enjoying being out in the sunshine. I could tell they enjoyed being where they were. I only observed them from afar. I did not recognize anyone in particular but could tell that they would welcome me if I approached. Yet, for some reason unknown to me, I did not walk over to where they were. I just stood there trying to think about what all had just happened to me. I was perfectly aware that I was still dreaming, yet aware of my streaming thoughts at the same time.

I somehow realized that even though I had been given the fabulous gift of self-love I still needed to see all these things. I needed to see the comparison of what people hold in their hearts and where this leads them to in realms beyond our own plane of existence.

Many, many thoughts went through my mind. I could feel the fabulous feeling of knowing that God did not judge me. Even though I felt myself less than worthy of his love He did love me. He accepted me as I am and I, in turn, knew that without having that same love for myself I could not fully understand how to give that love to others. How many times in my life had I heard about those truths? But I was never able to do or fully understand what they meant . . . until now.

I saw that God, in his withholding of judgment against us, lets us fall where we may. The more that we fall away from the spiritual love for ourselves and others, the more we fall away from God. He lets this be so and we experience what we choose to carry within our hearts.

This is very difficult to explain. Perhaps this is not what is true but this is what I felt, this is what I saw. Basically I completely know that our experience in the next realm will correspond with the level that our hearts find in this world.

When I awoke again, I was back in my room. Again there were tears on my cheeks. The light was on in my room. It was

4:30 in the morning. My dreams had lasted for many hours. Something in my heart told me that what had happened to me in the ambulance and in the hospital, both in and out of my coma, and what had just happened to me in these dreams were things I needed to go through. They happened at different times so that I would know that they were real. I had not been looking for any of this it all just happened. I felt as if an invisible circle of some sort was now complete.

Right then I needed to call my sister. I needed to hear her voice. I truly had so very much to think about.

MIRROR, MIRROR ON THE WALL

While I was a home recouping from the trauma I had several home health care people visit or check up on my progress. It just so happened that one of these visits was the day after my "blue room" dream. Bobbie, the home health care nurse, was sitting on a couch opposite me and was getting her laptop computer ready to enter details of my progress. We both heard a very loud crash coming from the kitchen. My husband, who was home sick in bed, Bobbie, and I, rushed to see what we all thought was someone perhaps throwing something heavy through the kitchen window.

We all looked around the kitchen for a moment, not daring to enter, for we couldn't see what had happened. Then we saw what it had been. An old antique mirror, which had been hanging on the far wall of the kitchen, had fallen to the floor. The hanger had somehow come out of the wall. My beautifully ornate mirror was now in many pieces and far beyond repair.

This isn't strange except that the mirror had been on the wall for about six years. It had been taken down and put back several times during our renovations of the house over the past few years. The hook it was on was well able to support the weight of the mirror. It had been secure in the wall. Yet here it was now on my floor, the hook had just simply fallen away from the wall taking the mirror with it.

Hubby headed back to bed as Bobbie and I stood and looked at the mess that needed cleaning up. I was still far too weak to do much of anything so Bobbie took the broom as I grabbed a trash can for disposal of all those pieces of glass. I was saying how I just couldn't understand how this could have happened. God had just given me, the night before, one of the most fabulous gifts of my life. (Earlier I had told Bobbie bits of my strange dreams the previous night.) Why would he now destroy one of my favorite things?

She was silent as she picked the fragments of mirror from the floor, then she asked me, "What did you use this mirror for?" I told her that since it was on the wall near the exit door to the kitchen that I always took one last look at myself before leaving the house. I would do the "check myself" routine to see if my hair was ok or my face looked as if it was ready to confront the world that day - typical woman stuff. A few more moments of silence and Bobbie turned to me and stated that perhaps God felt that I was Ok just as I am, and I didn't need to "check" myself anymore. I looked at her and silently agreed. Maybe this was God's way of finalizing my spiritual journey with a little earthly confirmation?!. Hmm.

THE LEARNING CIRCLE
OF LOVE

As time passed after my accident, I felt that I had so much processing to do inside of myself. The outside took care of itself. I was physically getting stronger every day. I had lots of rest, physical therapy, and the help of a loving family. Within two months my life, for the most part, returned to normal. Yet my inner self would never be the old normal I was before all of this transpired. How to understand what had happened to me?

Talking with some people certainly seemed to help. I know, at first, I was telling anyone I could about the wondrous things I saw and felt while in my coma. I was SO excited to tell everyone that God really did exist and I know that even though they seemed to share in my excitement, some people must have been silently shaking their heads in disbelief.

When I first returned home to rest and recover it seemed as if I was seeing the world with a pair of fresh new eyes. Everything was so new, so different to me somehow. I looked forward to each and every minute of the day. Waking, sometimes well before dawn, I would stand at the picture windows of our living room and watch the stars silently slip away as the majesty of a new day started to come alive, blossom, and unfold before my eyes. It was like I had never really experienced the beauty of each moment before and now I couldn't get enough! I was constantly in awe of what was before me. Magic seemed to be everywhere and my heart was in a constant state of gratitude. Simple things in life became glorious in their own right, and I relished living moment to moment, excited to see what would unfold. Each of those moments in their own uniqueness seemed to sparkle My husband did not quite know what to do with me. I was as excited as if I had just seen Martians land and was trying to tell the world that they were, in fact, real. I seemed to have the mind and voice of a child for quite some time. It was as if I had reverted to being very naive. Dan worried to the point of calling friends and discretely asking for advice. I am sure he wanted to know *"What do I do with her?"*

The days and weeks of my life carried me on. The old "Dea", was, in many ways, no longer there. How was I to integrate all this "knowing" that I didn't even know yet, into my new self? The world still outwardly looked the same yet was experienced and so very differently by me now. That new experience became my new vision. My new vision became my new reality, which in turn created even more new experiences. Somehow I had to make sense of it all. I knew I had been shown too much NOT to be changed from within. I couldn't yet wrap my thoughts around all the thoughts and pictures that swirled by me on a continuous basis now. I found myself looking at the world from two completely different planes of reality. I was having trouble morphing them together in a way that I could deal with and take forward in my life. At first I just wanted to get back to everyday life and get on with things. But little by little I found myself wanting to be alone with myself to somehow try and wade through it all to see what I could process and learn.

I don't actually know when I saw that circle again. I first felt the circle, as I described earlier, after waking from my blue room dream. At some point the clarity of why all this unfolded as it did hit me. It *was* a learning circle of sorts. My life before had been on automatic for many years. There was no searching for answers, no spiritual quests in my life for a very long time. I was just living day to day. I think that my experiences happened to me in the way that they did so that I would know that something beyond my little life, and bigger than the everyday real world, was trying to get my attention. Perhaps the process unfolded in increments so that ultimately I might be able to sort out the stages of learning so they might not be as easily dismissed by my skeptical mind.

The first jolt was the experience inside the ambulance. . . did I imagine it? Why would I? I was in a partial state of shock, terrified for the life of my dog. So why would I spend the time to conjure up "something" out of the blue, suddenly changing my whole demeanor and outlook on my emergency situation? It's not something that I can prove happened in this real world, yet I KNOW that it did. I think this happened to prepare me in a way for the "more" that was about to come. It was a slight opening of an inner door.

While in my coma, even though I cannot say where my soul was exactly, it certainly was conscious of existing without being attached to a body. And the depth of my soul knows that somehow I was being cared for by God. This journey opened me up to the LOVE that is coming from God, the LOVE that is here on earth, and the potential to LOVE within our souls. The door opened just a bit more. My visions on the hospital wall, led me to feel that all had culminated as it should, as it was meant to be. At home, the mirror falling to the floor when it did, seem to give me a bit of earthly confirmation about my thoughts...coincidence? Maybe. My blue room dream and even my few moments in the depths of ugliness were reconfirmations that came full circle. In my coma I had known the LOVE that God has for us. And later, in that blue room experience, I was shown again how much I am loved and that I can have that same love for myself.

Imaginings? Again I can prove nothing. The only proof I have is the growing of my heart, the changing of my soul, and the new world I am now slowly beginning to see with a new pair of eyes.

Yes, there was a circle, a circle that started with "God" slightly making himself known to me with that love and comfort in the ambulance, and coming full round when he opened my heart to love myself as he does. It took many months for me to see this and understand each segment of my journey. I know that I am only beginning to understand - there is so much more growth to come. So, the door had been fully opened and I passed through. A circle of lessons had come full round. How will it all unfold?

GOING FORWARD

It has been little over a year now since the accident, since the start of my journey. My words from here on are my attempts at winding my way through my thoughts to try to explain a bit of this new me. I am not a great thinker or intellectual. This is just me, trying to put into words, some of what I have found myself going through over these past months. Don't expect grandiose words of enlightenment, only the words of one small soul searching to somehow understand.

I was back fully into this life, yet had, and still have, the longing to go back to the light where I had been held. I wanted to feel again the intense love, understanding, and compassion that I knew were so much a part of the natural state of the other realm. I now knew that from the moment I first felt the tire of my car hit the rut in the road that November day, and all that followed, was somehow planned or destined to be. The interaction with the doctors, my family, dealing with everything this unexpected experience put before us, all of it seemed to be unfolding in an orderly succession of ongoing miracles. It seemed as if God was directing it all and all of it was perfect. It is hard to explain because in so many respects things were certainly not perfect. But didn't others see the miracles too?

In early 2009, just a short time after my accident and experience, I found myself with a great desire to start journaling my thoughts. Not a big deal in itself, but for me it was. I had never had the desire to journal or keep a diary as a youngster or as an adult. The words came slowly at first, not seeming to dare their way out of my brain and onto paper. I was definitely not comfortable looking at my own thoughts as they were written out before me. What could someone like me have to say that was worth much, if anything at all? The old haunts of inferiority still seemed to be with me. Something inside me however, told me to push through these feelings. I knew that we are all children of the Creator and there are no unworthy thoughts or feelings. I also knew now that nothing was hidden from the Universe. There are no hiding places, no secrets, all is bathed in light and knowing. So write I did. But I had no guidance in this effort. I found myself praying that the Creator might not leave me with these thoughts, not leave me to myself to understand them all. "Please don't leave me now," became my daily mantra.

So overwhelming, so very much to think about. What, just what, could I do with all of these thoughts streaming thought me? What could I even do with my life? Everything about any wants or desires had so totally changed. My priorities had certainly changed. I was aching inside of myself to get closer to God, do more for God, but "how?" or "what?" - I just didn't know. This was all totally new for me to be sure.

At some point in my thoughts, I realized that it is not what we accomplish here on earth that promotes us to greatness, rather that greatness abides in any act we do, no matter how trivial, if done with deliberate love. There is no better greatness than this. There is no other answer to what need be done. Every second of life should be like a prayer. I was understanding this little by little. Some days it seemed so easy to lean into the "Knowing". Other days I would feel as if it had all truly been a dream and I found myself in a lonely fog. As I wrote my thoughts during the days and weeks I wondered if it was when God whispered to my soul, that I would be wanting more. Does the Creator pick the time to talk to us? Does he pick the time that we will "choose" to hear his words? Never had I had such a desire to communicate, never have I felt so close to truly being alive.

SUN. APR 12: *I am listening and I know you have spoken to me. I may not understand much now, but with guidance and patience (on both sides) I know that my understanding will increase, and my ability to witness of such, will be in a way that will matter . .*

WEDS. APR 15: *What am I trying to figure out? What is it about living and being human that is so complicated? I sit here as the day unfolds, feeling the minutes wash by me. Today I just cannot find the words or thoughts that make any sense to me now. I cannot seem to get "it" right. Heck I don't even know what "it" is. Why am I stuck? You would think that our existence would be so easy to understand, we humans seem to want to mess it all up and make "being" so very complicated. The words seem to fall away from my mind. I need to just "be" a bit, and perhaps my head and heart will clear . . .*
...What can I do with the rest of my life that will make a contribution to this act of being human. I use to consider myself an artist, that is part of how I saw the person that I was. What will be my paint brush of the future? How do I break out of the mental box and old ways of thinking? Is this foolish to think that I even have anything worth saying?

In the still of my heart I know I will find the answers, know the meaning and direction will come, . . . Be patient Dea be patient.

SUN. APR 19: *I feel that everything we do, both verbally and with acts, needs to be our contribution to life, and to the Creator. How vividly I am aware of this now. Not just the prayers or good deeds that we do, are enough for what is ours to accomplish. Every breath we take, every minute of the day is HIS. We do not own claim to any of it . . . Living life needs to be a prayer in and of itself. The more we fall into the knowing of this, the more we will naturally do so. <u>Our lives must not be lived in gratitude of that which has been given. It must become the gratitude itself.</u>*

How could I deny what I had known to be realer than real for me in every way? I knew that my life had always been on a path of sorts. Yet now all the searching, stumbling along my wandering ways, were falling by the way side. I knew now that I had found the path. That I may lose my way from time to time, but the path itself would never be truly lost to me again. It will be my heart's desire to walk that path, and that desire, in and of itself will keep me on it, and ultimately in the light. The world is not all the flashy things we see, the real world is within the realms of our hearts and souls.

We are so very small in the scheme of it all. Yet each and everyone has a space that we alone fill. Even the smallest voice is heard by the universe, and the tiniest of thoughts ripples out from our souls as to cause an effect upon that universe. It is all a part of its weavings. How amazing!

Loneliness and fulfillment of one's soul are but a hair's width away from one another. These two states of being, exist side by side. The borders between the two though are always open. It is our choice, as to which side we decide to live within. It is that simple, and it is OUR CHOICE.

MON. APR. 20: *Whether I get "it" wrong or get "it" right, I know now my heart travels toward the light. And by doing that, going toward the light, even the wrong then becomes the desire for the right. I pray that I may use the gifts given me these past months in a way that will help others before my own journey comes to an end. I have been helped in a way far beyond measure, . . . Treasures of my heart now out shines any in the world outside myself. . . . My heart is at peace. Every day brings just a tad more understanding and even more desire for that understanding, and the knowledge to use it wisely . . . I know now that I must build a solid foundation inside my heart, for it is my heart I take with me to the next realm of being. I know that there is one, I know without a doubt that it exists.*

I think of how blessed we all are, yet how caught up in our own desires and dilemmas and frustrations, too. We cannot see what life truly is anymore. So caught up in the world and its trappings, we swim faster to stay with what is happening, yet what we really need to do is let go. The tides of light and truth will take us where we need to be. But I think we are always afraid to stop swimming. It is not the living of life which, I feel, is hard to do, but the constant act of letting go, when it is our very nature to cling and thrash and try to strive ahead. Letting go is such an opposition to what this hectic and unsettled world teaches us to do. I have found that by the mere act of letting go my life has actually become so very full. To me our understanding is like waves that rise and fall upon the shore, never constant for very long. That understanding or perception seems always a bit different and at times becoming ferocious and seemingly out of control: pure fury or daunting energy beating down the sands. Yet without the turbulent tides how would we know how cherished the calm silent soft ripples are when the world is right within our heart, when all is well?

MON. MAY 4: <u>Words not by me, but through me:</u>

What is there to say? The words flow forth like water, flowing as it knows how to do. Listen and be still . . . Listen. This is good timing for all, it is what you need to hear. You should not be afraid for I come to you, with love and understanding, this is so. If you give it time, you will understand. If you give it time, your heart will be opened. Yes, give it time and the love will flow, - Just ASK. For things to come and be, will be slow but the waters will still flow, it will not stop. Hear ME with your heart, Hear Me loud and clear. Many will fall away but this is to be, do not worry. If you listen, you will be told what the direction needs to be. The light ahead will be bright and clear, and those who walk in its light will forever be free . . .

LISTENING WITHIN
MY HEART

At times I find myself stopping to think about what has transpired within me. Of course the old "me" sometimes gets in there for a good bit of bantering between the sides of my being that are in conflict. The habit of "hanging on" still lingers inside, coming out to add conflict in the tussle for my soul. Yet with a few deep breaths and the stilling of my mind I can usually prevail with the new "me" and carry on from there. I am so filled with gratefulness now for what I have been given. Though I am still in the process of finding out what all that is. But in this new life, new heart of mine, I know that I am guided and will have the peace of soul that has eluded me for so very long. I know that I will not take one more day for granted, nor willfully hurt another with my words, thoughts, or deeds. I will gather strength in the "knowing" of what is right, and with my life, become a testament to that knowing.

It seems, looking back on it now, that I had prayed in vain almost my whole life, with only occasional answers. Or, maybe, I just wasn't listening to the answers I got. Yet it was enough to get me to here, and now, God has done the rest. So here I now am, so full, so at peace, grateful and bursting with wonderful thoughts and emotions. I will be dead and only ashes of what once was, in the not so distant future. Where will all this energy go? I hope to be added to the love and light I feel is out there. I KNOW I will not end with death.

So much to ponder in this little pea brain of mine. Fifty seven years old and embarking on a new adventure! How very cool is that?! There are so many blessings in my life, so much to be thankful for. I do thank God for giving me another chance to see all of this again, in such a different light. Almost dying does sometimes have its advantages!

SAT. MAY 9: I cannot resist a few more minutes being out on the deck in the sun. I sit sipping coffee, soaking in the morning warmth of that sun and the views of the valley below. The dryer hums just inside the kitchen door, with the soft sweet smell of clean clothes wafting out the vent and mingling with the fresh scent of the Pinon pines around me. Two or three different types of birds are chattering in the distance somewhere, and even the zzzzing insects are out and now complete the picture. The first hummingbird of the season reminds me I need to get a new house and food for them. I wonder if the "fake" owls we put up this past winter, will keep them away. I hope not. My dog meanders in the brush off the deck close by, my dear sweet, and very old kitty, also exploring the deck and its spring secrets. Some days it just all seems so very clear . . .

Yes I am so very different now than before. A new me lives inside. I love what is there, love what I see. My "blue room" experience showed me that I indeed was quite loveable! I find now I want to give, that of the gifts that were given to me. If I had only known how wonderful letting go would be. I had to truly die unto myself to learn how to truly live.

We seem to spend our whole lives searching for "The Answers." We read the many takes on the many different concepts of what life is. We could spend a lifetime reading, or going from seminar to seminar, or conference to conference. The quest for learning from the world outside ourselves is absolutely endless.

Some learn how to ring those spiritual bells, hum with vibrating crystal bowls, seek the wisdom of psychics, . . . the list goes on and on. We humans do like to make it all so complicated don't we? There is much to be said for all the learning from others and other sources, but worthless if we expect the answers to come from those things themselves and we do not use it for searching within. I had no idea that my journey would take me to the most simplistic place in the universe, a place called unconditional LOVE. I learned from it that I needed nothing but myself to get there, no books, no drums, no bells, nothing more than the willingness to let go and see that place, that IS LOVE, and ultimately . . . IS . . . GOD.

I know that I was not supposed to remember everything at once - the many things I learned or absorbed into my soul during my near death experience. I wouldn't have been able to handle it all. Yet in the quiet times of my heart, and little by little, snippets of knowledge come back to me, much of which I do not yet seem to have the words to write, or ability to convey. The knowing comes to me as I have the strength and openness to absorb. I was able to understand the miracle that each minute carries within itself. And each minute, and subsequent miracle is a destination in itself. So great are the things already here, existing in the here and now. Each minute becomes its own thing of beauty, woven into the next. Each minute, each miracle within, are the bridges to the destination my journey will lead me to.

MON. MAY 11: *I never have had the words before, to say what is truly inside my heart. Perhaps on this new journey of mine I will find them and use them as stepping stones to find my way home . . .*

I had spent many years thinking of myself as dysfunctional or hated parts of me for not living up to whatever it was I felt I should have been. I know that at times I even hated myself for thinking I had nowhere to fit in this world, nothing special to contribute. My perception of self kept changing. Yet now I know that I was never really dysfunctional, just human, and searching. And throughout all of it, I was still very much loved by the ONE who creates, the one who creates through LOVE. I seem to have beat myself up almost my whole life to learn something I already knew somewhere deep inside but never wanted or was able to accept. How dumb can one be for so very long? How simple the answers become when I can let go of my own thoughts for one bit to let the real truth find its way to my heart. Is there any way I can pass this onto others? I was so very blessed to have been given a chance to have the journey that I did, I feel it would be wrong not to share. God had whispered to me that he would take care of me, . . . and that he certainly did. I was given back my life, as it was meant to be. I choose to give it back with Love 100%.

Part of that is now writing what I felt, saw and experienced, and sharing it as I can. Maybe there is something in all of this for someone else too.

WED. MAY 13: *Where are you taking me now God?.....I have lost sight of the land and I journey now in the vastness of my unknown. Yet I am so at peace with it all. For even though I don't know where I am, or where I am going, I know that I an not lost . . . letting go, letting go!*

THURS. MAY 14 11 p.m.: *I am almost bursting with the quiet excitement inside of me now. I am still reeling from the fact that this wonderful experience happened to me! ...Would I have ever gotten to this place if I had not gone through my November journey? ......I don't know . . . Every day is more beautiful than the day before - How can this be possible? I truly do love myself now. All those years, geesh how many? ...that I had at best made a truce with my soul. " Don't look at it too much Dea, and you won't find much to hate about yourself," So I didn't. I could always keep myself on a somewhat even keel if I just didn't examine "me" too closely. It was how I could make it through life, and somehow the years just added up. . . . Now, my heart is in a rush, and bursting to see what it can do, in repayment for this new life that has been given me. I don't own claim to any of it, not one hair on my head, or breath that I take. I feel the unseen . . . I feel the power, the energy behind our lives. For the very first time I know what it is to believe, - no to "know" . . . Believing isn't just the acknowledgment that there is a creator . . . it's the breathing in and becoming one with HIM. Then you "Know." And when you open your eyes in unison with HIS, the world is not the same one you existed in before . . . or can ever go back to . . . Contentment, Happiness, . . . Happy to be Content, Content to be Happy . . . it all feels so very good!*

FRI. MAY 15 – 3:00 a.m.: *Cannot sleep, and the words are flowing:*
I Felt It Would Happen Someday
We bow to one another, you softly take my hand.
We step into each other's arms, and dance away in music, to an unseen land.
You look deep into my eyes, to see what lingers there.
You see my love looking back at you – no worries, no cares.
I look into yours, I see exactly the same.
The Love, The Joy, The Feeling with no name.

With your arms around me, we slowly drift across the floor.
Our Hearts melt together, and I feel myself no more.
For we have come together in this dancing in the night.
Two hearts as one, slowly whirling – whirling towards the light.

The universe, our dance floor, lit by a million shining stars.
The music, I think, must be angels, singing from afar.
I know now, I can go on forever – this dancing with me and you.
I felt it would someday happen – always something that I knew.

Thank you for tapping me on the shoulder that wondrous   and beautiful night.
I smiled - said YES – I knew that it was right.
I felt it would someday happen – always something that I knew.
Your love for me unending, as mine is now for you.
I felt that it would someday happen, always something that I knew.

Thank you God for asking.
Thank you through and through.
That I would someday dance forever
Knowing it would surely be with you.

Now I understand.

Looking back on this first poem of mine, I am amazed how quickly and easily the words seemed to flow. Though not a great poem in the scheme of literary workings, it was to the "T" where my feelings were at that very moment in time. And for me, it has captured perfectly where I was that late spring night in May - alone with God

SAT. MAY 16: *"Ask and it will be refilled" . . . that is what you told of my heart, . . . did you really mean it? I think from the peace that has found its way there that you did . . . Thanks! :-)*

SUN. MAY 17: *Questioning who I am, or where I am going? And what is all this for?, are questions I know I can let others ask for themselves now, let others worry about in their own way. For I know none of that matters . . . it is what it is, we are what we are, and it will be what it is to be . . . if we just take care of adjusting our own hearts to receive your love, and pass it through to others, I know that you will take care of the rest . . . In the letting go - I find both you and me again. You have always been there though I did not see. You were there with as much love for me as always . . . Thank you God, I think I can sleep now.*

TUES. MAY 26: *My breaths are my gifts that have been given me, . . . I give them back in Love, Service, Devotion, & Dedication to the power that graced me to breathe at all! . . .Thank You, Thank You Thank You!*

WED. JUN. 3: *I feel as if I am waiting your return, yet I know that the opposite is the truth. You are always there and patiently waiting for me . . .*

I am still in awe of this new part of me that has opened up. I don't think I can ever remember a time I would have been so willing to put what was kept in secret places within my heart, open now for all to see. I would have never been willing to openly talk about spirituality to those I did not know. Heck, I have had trouble speaking about such things to people I did know. Yet here I am in whatever feeble form it takes, baring my thoughts for all. It is a new experience for me for sure. I had been somehow "told" that I would be doing things I had never done before, perhaps this is why I feel so led to try and get these words out. But I know that I will follow this feeling and these urges to finish my thoughts in a way that I do ultimately feel comfortable sharing with others. When I think about what has transpired over these many months I find myself giving thanks that I did not miss what I think I was supposed to hear, see, and know. How terribly sad it would have been to not have been aware, and all of this pass me by. How even more sad for me, had I not made the choice to learn from so great a gift that had been given to me. At times I feel as if there is so little time left to get things done. I don't even know what all those "things" are, yet all the time in the world if needed will be there as planned. The weaving of life will be as it should be.

People have asked me if I "saw" God or Jesus while having this incredible near-death experience. To that I have to say in the literal term of recognizable earthly beings and shapes - NO. But do I know that another realm exists? Yes, without a doubt, without a doubt. I did not see them in figures but do know that I was in a realm created by them, for us, in love - a Love so vast and unending in its very nature. I feel that we do not have to have a near death experience to see that realm for I know it is here, within our hearts, for each and every soul upon the world today. Much like Dorothy's words in the Wizard of Oz . . . "We don't have to look any further than our own backyards to find our hearts' desire."

I was just given a chance within my life to see around myself for a brief instant, to get to where I needed to be. I was able to let "me" stand aside, let fall the pride, arrogance, ignorance, stubbornness, and all the rest that I had used to navigate within this world of mine. For just a bit I was lucky enough to somehow have the privilege of having all that wiped away so that I could "see" what truly was there waiting. The LOVE was what I found. In that love, that "knowing", I found that we are all capable of having that same love. If we, for just one short brief instant, still our hearts and ask we will be filled with the essence of what we truly are. It is so very true, that the true Kingdom is inside our hearts, it has and always will be so.

FRI. JUNE 26: *It is still dark out yet a few birds have started to chirp their morning Hellos . . . My heart is bursting, my tears have flowed, and my Thank You to YOU, just don't seem to be enough. What can I do? What will be my calling? You weave us all together God, it is your will and only yours that moves the seas of life. In these brief quiet times I can catch sight of how miraculous it all is! How glorious the structure of the human spirit and its interactions with each other are. Each moment in itself is a miracle unfolding unto the next. We must not move so fast that we do not catch it. Let our minds be in the "knowing" of each of those moments of life, to be aware of all that goes on before us, to all that we may receive if we are paying attention. How awesome it all is . . . YOU have remade me, and in YOU I have become whole! ....How many birds have found their voices in these past five minutes as I write? Both windows of the bedroom open. I am getting to hear their songs in stereo. How cool!*

SUN. JUNE 28: *Today is another day, ready to be explored, lived, and soon to be a memory upon the future pages of my soul . . . What will happen on this day? How will it all unfold? Who will walk before my eyes? Will you grace me with the gift to "see?" , I hope so. Many paths will cross mine, many people will come into this little world of ours, into the store, interact with us* and be on their way. How many threads will be woven today, or foundations set for the building of tomorrow? .....How much can I do? How much can I give? .... Words have not said it all, nor have I been able to give words as well as I could to the thanks that is within me. But you know, you know what is there inside my heart. .. Thank you to the universe. I am so very small, yet still you know that I am there, and that there is a place for me somewhere, all is as it should be.

MON. JUNE 30: *I am seeing how important realization is to our lives. It is through any type of realization that we can acknowledge miracles, and the small daily unfolding that are those miracles. They are not of us - but of HIM. How we react to them, is of us. The more realization we have that HE IS complete source of everything, even our choices, we will ultimately make the right ones . . . For the realization that God, Creator, Source of All, does only good, gives us the realization that there is indeed a plan, a source, one that we are not in control of, or ever could hold accountable. Realization that Source is always right, leads me to the realization that ALL, no matter what, is ultimately good. It is only those that accept the" badness" of something as a reality, does that then become the realization of same, creating the separation from Source, or God. The "bad" now becomes to us real. ... My heart, my mind and my soul need guidance, and I know that placing my faith in Source or God, all will then fall into place as it should. I realize I need to diminish my own thoughts of what I want, want to be, or how things should be done. I need to learn to leave that up to HIM that created me. I open my heart to the "knowing" more of the miracles of life that surround me, so that I may do more as my gift back to Source . . . I ask for the gift of open "eyes" to see, an open heart to "receive," and an "open mind " to the realization of the truth.*

WED. JUL 1: *I am so willing to do more . . . I pray that I will be guided in a direction that will give me the fullness of purpose that I seek . . . Yet life cannot be better that it is right now. For it all just "IS" Even if circumstances were in my personal judgment, to be better than this, they would still be just "IS" My personal task is to keep that in close remembrance and to stop* *many times where I stand, and give . . . Thanks for the perfection of each moment....It is so true that wherever our energies or desires lie, there too will be our heart. My prayer tonight is that all my energies be given back to YOU, the ONE who has blessed me with the abilities to do anything in the first place. I do not own any of my breaths, I had to have them almost totally taken away to realize that fact. It is in that recognition and realization that I have found "my road" to the final path that leads to home, that leads to God, my heart is happy with that thought, - Goodnight.*

When I sometimes stop to take a look at what has transpired over these past months, I can give myself quite a start. Did I ever in a million years think that I would have my views on reality and the truths of that reality change by what seemed like a few dreams? I certainly did not! I had always acknowledged the possibilities of happenings beyond our worldly existence, but never did I imagine that experiencing it would happen to me. Over and over again I come back to the stillness in my heart and I know that it is real for me. I was led to "Know" that I did indeed have a purpose. That purpose may be to just live my life, for the glory of the one who made me. The peace I have inside my heart now is such a physical thing, a physical feeling. I feel like a child who only knows trust in a parent. I feel, too, that it is not for me to ponder over too much. It seems as if every day some small discovery happens for me to take on my journey forward.

I found that happiness is not something to look for, it is not, or ever has been outside of me. Happiness is what you are, is what you can be with what you have. Happiness is not a destination, but a state of being. Any of us can have it at any time, any time in our lives. All we have to do is let it in. How have I been so blind for so long to something so very simple in its nature to do? I don't think life was intended to be as complicated as it has become, as we have made it. I think we, as humans, have made it difficult on ourselves because we have fallen away from the simplicity of being. We have fallen away from acknowledging Source, the very Source that created us. At least I know that I have and I do see a lot of the world that seems to have done the same.

I feel that each one of us takes away our own understanding from everything that happens within this life, whether to us personally or to the world as a whole. We each operate on different levels of intellect, comprehension, and interpretations of what that life is. There is only one encompassing source of Creation, yet I feel that there are untold millions of roads that lead to Him. Each of us is at a different place within our minds, our hearts, and our abilities to understand.

"When God whispers in your ear," to paraphrase author Max Lucado, "and calls your name," it is on a level, of understanding, meant just for you, that you are "knowing" at that given time. The source meets us where we are. The world and its occupants operate on so many levels of intelligence and understanding, yet God comes to each as we need, so that we are able to hear and understand. But hearts must be open to receive what is needed at that time. We all do have a choice to open ourselves to the knowing and the light . . . or not.

AUG.4: *My heart and soul are where I will find my life's worth. It is not outside me. Tuning into the essence of what comes* *into my heart when open to God, is where all the answers, peace and love will be found. ...looks like another beautiful day and with my soul set to sail, all will be as it is meant to be . . . and that is good.*

AUG. 9: *Lead me as you will, give me the ability to serve with the life I now have . . . for those are the roots that take hold and spread within the fertile soil. The sands and dust of not Knowing or not wanting to Know will be swept away with the winds, with it too, those that choose to keep their hearts closed . . . every second is a new chance to become a new person. God gives us opportunities, and with them we create our earthly lives, while building our heavenly lives from what we create with those opportunities . . .*

AUG 19: *I can see a new shore that I have never set foot on before. I look out into the sun on the edge of the far horizon. The waves are softly lapping at the shoreline, and at my feet where I now stand. The waters are dark, yet I feel warmth. In the unknownness of those darkened waters, I still feel the comfort and protection of God. For a few brief moments I can feel the soft salty breezes surround me, smell the ocean's briny scent and the crispness of a new day. I give thanks for this moment and know that when I turn to walk away, I am home.*

FRI. AUG 21: *Still, is what today is. It is like life is holding its breath to see what will happen next. Sunny, cloudless, and still. ...If I get lost in my mind, will you find me?...if I stray from the path and find myself in the woods of darkness and chaos, will you see me? ...If I stumble and fall and find myself on my knees, will you lift me up again so that I may once more walk upright? ... If my heart wanders, not in deliberate waywardness, but like that of a child following some beautiful butterfly that distracts and mystifies, will you still love me and guide me back home? ... if I become empty and lonely of heart and soul, will you not fill me back to overflowing with love? ...If I give my heart and soul and life to you will you not show me what I need to do . . . show me my life's purpose? For there is no other purpose than to serve. You have brought me too far for me to go back to as I once* *was . . . Will you show me what I am capable of doing? ...I know that I am ready, my heart tells me you think so too, . . . thanks.*

AUG. 25: *I can sometimes sit the night away enjoying all its magic. It is in this still of these late nights that I can find Him, feel closer to Him. For a time the world and everything in it seems to be understood, loved in but a brief clarity, that sometimes fades with the dawn. Yet sometimes lingers on . . . to help me with my day.*

AUG. 30: *It is not the creator that waxes and wanes, it is I. Secure and centered one day, nerves jumbled, and mind askew the next. Dear God please help me center myself today . . . it is true, when our perception of a thing changes, that very thing itself will change. All is only how we perceive it to be. So when confronted with a shift in view, or feeling about something, perhaps the way the day is going, the perception must be changed in order for that day to also change in compliance with that perception . . . yes we do make our own worlds. ...but today I give thanks for my getting to this point, for my gift of self love, and inner growth and strength . . . May I learn to shine where I stand, to shine in the glory of how YOU see us, and what we all have the potential to be . . . Thank you for bringing me closer to home. :-)*

" Surely goodness and mercy shall follow me all the days of my life":
-PSALM 23:6

SEPT. 3: <u>Words not by me, but through me:</u>*When in doubt give all your fears to ME. look no longer for what you seek, for it is here. It now has a home within the wall and lands of your heart. Gone is the last of not Knowing, for now you are one with ME . . . Dark of night gives way to the Knowing, and light within your soul. Sing songs of long ago, and forever keep the word as it was meant to be. See now for you shall Know, but no words will be spoken, other that which bears across the heart. The soul shall seek Me, and I shall be found. Close your eyes and see Me for what I am . . . LOVE.*

SEPT: 18: *It is not quite fully dawn, yet the sky is light, but not yet hit the valley floor. The living room window slightly open so I can tell by the wafting cool breeze that fall is on the way. The room feels cool and crisp. Yellow has come to the other side of the valley, I can see this outside my window as I write. Patches of that yellow gold dot the hillsides and the valley floor too is dotted with the gold changing that it will soon pass on to others. Leaves blow across the streets, and you can hear the low swirling sound of the wind. Where will I go today? How will my day unfold? ...I leave it to YOU to lead me as you will. Thank you for another day . . . They all seem so very precious to me now.*

BEGINNING TO UNDERSTAND

Not all my days have been filled with light and love. Confusion and distractions of old ways keep me down sometimes. I feel as if I don't have the energy to fight them, or feel as if that "spark" of understanding is gone somehow. I don't like those days very much to be certain, nor can I always "wish" them away no matter how much I center myself.

Life has ways of blind-siding us. We feel firmly planted in ourselves, in our knowing, and, in an instant, it seems to have vanished. We wake up to the loss of a loved one, or sickness and injury. Or we find we are adrift in the sea of turmoil that the world has somehow created for us. I sometimes get thrust to my knees with the overwhelming heartaches of this world. I am slammed to the ground and as if God himself had jammed his fingers inside my chest and ripped my heart out by the roots. All that is left is an empty shell, not yet dead, but certainly not alive. The year has seen some of those days, my sister lost her beloved, companion and pet Chipper. I have lost a few friends to death, watched helplessly as others battled great illnesses, and, of course, financial woes seem to always be lurking right around the corner. The list of woes seems to go on and on.

MON. SEPT 28: *(The morning after the accidental death of Sandy's little dog Chipper) . . . Sis is still asleep as I write today. I have spent the night at her house to keep her company, or just be close at hand during her time of grief. The sun is slowly* *lighting the valley sky now. I can only see a small portion of that land and sky from Sandy's living room chair where I sit. No clouds dot the sky and the colors get brighter with each passing moment. It feels strange to watch a new day unfold from a new perspective, and not from my bedroom at home. I haven't wanted to check in on her yet, as not to disturb what little sleep I am sure she is getting. I hear the passing cars outside on the highway increase in numbers as the day takes hold. another day will be in full swing. I listen to the pendulum clock in her kitchen. It pays attention to nothing and no one. It has only one obligation, to keep the tick tock sound beating off the seconds as they pass. God please lay your hand across her heart today, losing a pet, a special pet, is no different a degree of loss than that of losing a loved one . . . I know that you see the hurt that is there.*

Each of us are all so different in our way of learning. How many different ways must you know God, to reach each of us as we need?

....My sleeping dog, the tick tock of the clock, and the soft humming of the house, are all that keep me company as I wait for sis to awaken and for the day to begin. I sit and wait for YOU to whisper in our hearts.

......sleep well little friend Chipper, you were, and still are, very loved.

TUES. SEPT. 29: *Life and death, beauty in both, yet the intensity of it all sometimes seems to crush our very souls. Oh how daunting to love so, to hurt, to feel. Leaning into those feelings of life, can rip the heart from the body. Oh God . . . why does being human and alive sometimes have to ache with the most gut wrenching feelings imaginable? ...... The merry go round of emotions bring their own set of feelings, frustrations, and longings, . . . how can a heart stand it all?*

I know that I was given a glimpse of enlightenment, though only brief, before the trappings of this world covered it over. And true it was for only the shortest of moments in the scheme of things. But it only took that flicker to change my being, and my soul. I may never get back to that same place, while here on this earth, yet I KNOW that it is there, and but a breath away. The Knowing in my heart has somehow changed the person that I was, into the person I am striving to be. I don't need facts. I have all the proof I need within myself now. By surrendering into that "Knowing" it will provide all that I ever need or will be. I so look forward to the days ahead.

I know also, that this God is not something that is "up there," "out there" or "over there." He is not there, while we are here. He lives among us now, and always has. He is not something to pray "to" or "at" or keep at a distance while we go on with the making of our own lives. God is always "right here." It is we who wander, whose thoughts make the divide. It is we who do not want or do not choose to seek the right level of understanding to feel his presence.

I think we wait for God to do something, whether it's to touch our hearts, heal a wound, or make life "right." I feel we have a tendency to wait for him to do these acts, when in truth I feel that it is we who must do the changing. He is always here, always healing, loving and making things right. Life is always right, it is we and our ways that disturb the perfection that is God's doing. One way we can change is by opening up to the fact that he IS within us all the time. By acknowledging the essence of that, all else within us, will then change.

I know that many times in my life I felt that God, or Source, had "let me down". I felt that I had surrendered in a way I thought was right, but still things did not happen for what I thought was the best.. Was God trying to teach me a lesson, or punish me perhaps? But now I have the understanding that life, no matter how it happens, is still perfect as it is. It is I and my thoughts that make judgments as to what I feel is perfect or not. This, then, becomes what might be a slanted look at the perfection that is still there beyond my own limited judgment or vision. I feel that, many more times in my life than I would like to admit, I have not put my mind and heart to that openness to know, see or feel the full power of what God is giving us all the time . . . perfection.

It is like finding that needle in the haystack, or the 'sweet spot" of existence, when I can see, feel and know God most. The gate, I know, is always open. It is always there and available to us. And once found it is truly vast, wide and welcoming. But we must fine tune the radar of our hearts, minds and souls to pass through to the other side. Without that understanding, or desire to have it, we will never find our way through the rock-laden waters of existence to find the safe harbor -the harbor that offers rest, peace and love of God. Once we do find that level of knowing all else becomes unimportant since the light and that harbor become the only desired and attainable end. The end is becoming one with the light, one with God.

I would have to say, that I feel that we are the ones who make that attainable end hard to reach. A lifetime of dealing with worldly things, wants, desires, and perceived needs, give us the false security that they are what matter most. For even in death I feel our souls will search and wander, with empty fitful desires, if we are found still hanging onto the earthly attributes of our egos. Our earthly lives are spent building up the "I' or "me" of ourselves. Yet it is only when we finally let that go that we can see the spirit of universal existence. To give up one's self completely is to surely finds oneself in full.

I do not possess the grandiose words to illuminate how I feel, or what I have felt these past many months. But now I have been able to write my own simple words of what has happened to me. I still long for direction and find myself having to calm down the impatience inside of me. For now I know that what is to be is not of my timing at all but is that of the One who created me. I have found that surrender is the key - the letting go of self, of will, and of wants. These are part of what is necessary to be truly guided. The more I lay claim for myself, the more I realize that is not the way. Letting go, is the key to getting ALL.

OCT. 1: 2 a.m. <u>Words not by me, but through me:</u> ... *There is an understanding now I believe will serve you very well . . . understand this, it is all for a reason. When I am nigh, you will know in your heart. Give Me your love, give me your light, and all will be well. Never let go, never give up for all is the way it needs to be . . . You can understand with your heart when you hear Me call. When there is pain, when there is sadness, let yourself go into the light and I will be there. Always give me love, always it will be returned. Yes, it will always be returned. Then you are one with me, then you are part of the All, forever and always.*

(From me) . . . there is comfort in the night. The sanctuary of my room protects my thoughts. I float into the universe and back sometimes with ease. Is it a longing, a desire, a deep-rooted passion that takes hold? Once you know what is there, once you know what exists, how can anything ever be the same again? .... the world outside holds so much turmoil. Why do people not still their hearts? Why does evil seem to prevail? How much better is this peace inside one's heart! ....In the stillness of this night it's almost as if I can feel all those who now and before me, have also found the spot in our hearts, that knows the true quiet, the true peace, and the true Love. My strength comes from that which is invisible inside myself, that which has opened my self to lean into the "knowing" - into God.

Oct. 21: 10:15 p.m. *Tonight I am in the calm of my soul. I sit here with pen in hand feeling so close to God. I realize now that nothing can take the place of these silent moments when I can feel that closeness with him, fully knowing nothing in the world matters more than turning my heart in the right direction. I may not always hear the words, but I know deep within that he is here. So tonight I sit and get back to myself, back to HIM, and back to Love. . . . Thank you God, Goodnight.*

In this past year I have felt closer to knowing me, loving me, and loving where I stand, than in any other time in my entire life. It is as if all the worldly garbage just dropped from view and the world is now shiny and new. I cannot fully articulate the words which would give true description to the depths of how I feel. But these past pages are my attempts at doing so. These many months I have been growing into that newness of learning and into the new reality it has created. A lifetime of doubt and fears still find their way into my mind from time to time. Yet I can see most of them now for what they are, and surrender them to the light. I have been given such wonderful gifts yet I can only keep them if I give them away - they are not whole unless they are divided and shared. I think that "knowing" God can happen in an instant. Growing into Him, however, takes time. I am so very grateful for having been given both.

Also the past year since my experience has seemed to have gone by very quickly. I must admit I have enjoyed the process of talking either to myself on paper, or contemplating with God. It has been a journey I have cherished, and learned from as well. I like the me that I have finally become and I know there is still much to do and learn along my path. I wait and know that even in my waiting guidance is there. I know that I am truly loved, that I indeed love me, and now I can fully reach out to love and share with others.

There is nothing you need to do but put the quick fixes of this world aside, open your heart in honesty, and desire, and in HIS time, he will come to you in answer . . . and LOVE.

TO YOU

I hope that I have somehow shared a portion of what I have experienced in a way that might possibly give you even a moment's cause for reflection. The most important thing I found out for me personally is that this Creator lives not only OUT there somewhere but inside of me and my soul. God is the Creator and I am the "created" - a creation that is held in love and light. When I lean into that knowledge nothing else matters for the way of my life and growth will then unfold as it was meant to do. These words I have been led to write are new to me yet I find they are starting to come with ease. Thank you for reading.. . .I Thank God, for giving me those words I was able to find within my heart.

... Little by little, the dark moves a bit further away. The circle of light around my heart grows stronger . . . I strive to keep that heart open, for in doing so I can see how perfect this existence is, and always will be . . . To see that is to somehow see the face of God.

Love Forever, . . . Dea

If you indeed cry out for insight, and raise your voice for understanding: . . . then you will . . . find the knowledge of God.
--Proverbs 2:3,5

There is no way to put a price on what I have learned and so I have made my story available through donations only. At present it costs about $5.00 per book to produce. Any donations received will certainly be appreciated and will go toward future printing costs.

I am pleased to send copies to you for your family or friends but I do need compensation for the actual media shipping charge. I would love to send them all out for free, but alas! Donald Trump I am not.

If you feel that my book has something worth sharing with others I would love for it to be passed along rather than simply sitting on a bookshelf and I Thank You in advance for doing so. I set this free, like a butterfly, to go wherever the winds of life will take it.

More importantly, I would love to hear your thoughts and share feelings or outlooks. Please feel free to email me or you can go to my blog diary of sorts, to contact me or make a post. Again I say Thank You for letting me share with you the wonderful journey I was allowed to experience.
God Bless!

Dea Dewitt-Maltby

Email: itsluckie@msn.com
Blog: Wordstomysoul.blogspot.com